Guided Imagery
with Children

Successful Techniques
to Improve
School Performance
and Self-Esteem

Guided Imagery with Children

Successful Techniques to Improve School Performance and Self-Esteem

Sarah Berkovits

Whole Person Associates
Duluth, Minnesota

Whole Person Associates
210 West Michigan Street
Duluth, MN 55802-1908
800-247-6789

Guided Imagery with Children

Printed in the United States of America

10 9 8 7 6 5 4 3 2 1

ISBN 1-57025-214-9

Library of Congress Control Number: 2004109872

Author photo courtesy of Nikibi Studio

Dedication

For Colette,
my teacher of imagery and life

Table of Contents

Acknowledgements

I should like to thank the many students I have been privileged to work with in three continents over the past twenty-five years. They have taught me resilience, perseverance, and joie de vivre, come what may.

Thanks to my mother for her support and for believing in me in her very quiet and modest way. Thanks to my sisters, Bella, Yaffa, and Miriam, and my brother, Berel, for their ongoing interest and support. I am particularly indebted to my sister Leah who brought her vast skill and expert touch to the proofreading of the manuscript.

Thanks to my publisher, Carlene Sippola, and editor, Susan Rubendall, for making the trip such a pleasant one, and to Amanda Materne for her help with organizing the material.

I wish to express my appreciation to Rainelle Burton, Judy Wilkinson, Bea Sheftel, and my many other friends and teachers at the International Women's Writers Guild, too numerous to mention by name.

Especial thanks to Tisha Graham: your amazing generosity has touched me deeply, and your wise comments and feedback have been invaluable to me. I treasure your friendship.

A very special thanks to Jean Zipser, Angela Tahaan, and Pearl Lam for so generously taking the time to read and comment on the manuscript. Thanks also to Yitta Halberstam for her ongoing support and friendship, to Priscilla Chavez-Reilly and Cristina

Casanova for enabling me to introduce imagery work into the New York public school system, and ultimately to the Jewish and Catholic school systems of New York.

Thanks to Gerald Epstein, M.D., for sharing his typist with me, and to Bernice Linder, my other typist, who was always ready to meet my deadlines.

Thanks so much to Dr. Maurice Lipsedge, a tower of strength and brilliance, and Dr. Brian Koehler, a wise and humble friend, and a real mensch.

Special thanks to Denise Kenny for your unconditional love, generosity of heart and soul, and beautiful letters and cards. You are truly an incredible human being. To know you is to love you.

To my dear friend Leah Mark: Words cannot express what your friendship means to me. For your unswerving loyalty and ongoing encouragement and support, I thank you from the bottom of my heart.

Last but not least, thanks to Colette, my mentor for the past twenty-three years, who told me to write this book, and who never ceased to believe in me. You have helped me transcend multiple obstacles and taught me "to see at first the good."

Introduction

"Imagination is more important than knowledge."

—Albert Einstein

"What's imagination? When you look into your mind and see pictures — that's imagination."

—Michael, age 7

What is Guided Imagery?

Several years ago, I approached the teacher of a fifth-grade class and asked her if any children in her class were in danger of being held back at the end of the year. She mentioned a boy by the name of Gary, and when I asked her why he might be held back, she said he was failing everything. I happened to be acquainted with Gary, and I didn't understand why he was failing. To me, he seemed to be an intelligent boy: sensitive, poetic, and articulate. He was also a thinker, asked thoughtful questions, had a great imagination, and was something of an artist, too. I asked the teacher, "Why is he failing everything?"

She said, "Because he never finishes an assignment."

I asked if I could see Gary for counseling and left the room muttering under my breath, "I'll be damned if Gary will be held back." Next morning, bright and early, I had Gary in my room. "Gary," I said, "how would you like to do an imagination game?"

He nodded his assent.

"To play this game," I continued, "we have to close our eyes. Sometimes, when we close our eyes, we see pictures in our mind's eye. So sit comfortably in your chair, close your eyes, and breathe out slowly through your mouth three times." I paused for him to breathe out, and then I continued, "See yourself in a race. What kind of a race is it?"

"It's a bike race," he said.

"Hear the whistle go off signaling you to start. Do you hear it?" I inquired.

"Yes, yes, I hear it," Gary replied excitedly.

"Can you tell me how many people are in the race, what's happening, and where you come in at the end of the race?"

"There are fourteen other people in the race," said Gary. "I'm pedaling very fast. Faster than the others. I come in second."

"And how do you feel?" I inquired.

"Wonderful," he replied, with a broad grin on his face.

"Good," I said. "Now go back to class, quickly. I'll see you again some other time." With that he left my office. As he closed my door, I noticed he was all but dancing out of the room.

At lunchtime, I heard a knock on my door. I got up to open it and there was Gary, holding his book wide open in his hands. In prominent red letters his teacher had written, "Gary finished his assignment today!" After that, Gary continued to complete his tasks both at home and in school, and his grades went up steadily. Upon my recommendation, he attended summer school to catch up on his learning deficits, and in September he moved up to the sixth grade with the rest of his class.

When I won the race It helped me to do better in School, because I kept thinking about the race. It made me do better in school, because I realized that school was the race were I had to win frist or second place.

Wining the race in my mined made me believe in my self.

I chose to put Gary in a race because that was the image that came to me when I asked myself, "What will help him work faster?" The exercise was simple, quick, fun to do, and it worked. It saved Gary's parents thousands of dollars in tuition, and it saved Gary from the humiliation, embarrassment, and shame of being held back. Rejection, in this case holding someone back a grade, generally doesn't work. If anything, it creates more problems. What does work is success. I am convinced that the good feelings that accompany success act as powerful motivators for further success. We can understand why it is that a child who fails keeps failing again and again: he simply doesn't have the good feelings needed to motivate him to keep trying. Instead, he carries the burden of failure and all the painful emotions accompanying it— lowered self-esteem, the belief that I'm no good, I don't count for much, I'll never be able to please, they don't love me, I'm stupid, I'm dumb, I'm ugly—the list goes on and on. Feelings of self-deprecation and fear of rejection can't fuel the fires of enthusiasm and confidence necessary for success.

Sherry

I like this Image class
because it is fun, you can exercise
~~you~~ your mind, you can expres
your self more clearly, you can
lern how to do creative writing,
and you can expand your mind.
You can also lern more about
life. Insted of some one telling
you about life you can
explan it to them on
a peace of paper. You fell
~~prou~~ prund and you have
more belife in your self

Age: 10

So we have to ask ourselves how we can help failing children succeed. The best way that I know is through guided imagery. Because imagery depends on imagination in which all is possible— unlike rationalism which sets limitations—children can easily visualize themselves succeeding, and when they do this they get to experience the wonderful feelings that go along with success. This happens before they've actually done anything. We know that the brain doesn't distinguish between an imaginary experience and the same experience in concrete life. We see this from our dreams at night. For example, in our dreams, when we are being chased and run away, our bodies actually sweat; our heartbeat becomes more rapid; we get out of breath and experience fatigue. And so it is with anything else we dream about. If it is something sad we cry, something frightening we scream, something funny we laugh, and so on. Our bodies respond to the imagined experience with physiological changes that can actually be measured scientifically.

This book, which harnesses the potential of imagery, is a powerful new tool for parents and for professionals who work with children.

Guidance counselors, teachers, social workers, and psychologists will find it especially useful. And bright children can work with it on their own or with friends. It can stimulate self-awareness, help develop interpersonal skills, assist with understanding feelings, and show children how to use undiscovered inner resources. The power of this book lies in the fact that it is at one-and-the-same time diagnosis, prognosis, and cure.

The book can help children of all ages, as well as grownups who have not lost touch with their inner child. It is based on a new approach which educators and parents will find inspirational and useful. I have found this approach particularly useful for teachers in managing their classrooms and maintaining discipline, providing more time for actual learning.

The idea for this book came to me when I saw how powerful guided imagery exercises were in effecting change in people's lives. I noticed with amazement the ease with which change can occur, how painless it can be, and how widely available transformation is through this method. I wanted to make guided imagery universally accessible so all could experience its beneficial effects.

It is my fervent hope and dream that parents and teachers will find this book useful in helping their children grow into happy individuals who are able to succeed in all areas of their lives.

The Nature of Children
"Do grownups also have imagination, or only children?"

—Jeff, age 7

Working with images comes naturally to children. As one eight-year-old girl reported to me, "People say I'm the weirdest, brightest child they've ever met. You see, I sometimes become two people: the pupil and the teacher. When the pupil part of me doesn't know the answer, I become the teacher. Now that I'm the teacher, I know the answer so I write it down and get it right."

It has been my observation that children do not like to talk about their problems or even admit that anything is bothering them. They will deny or avoid rather than discuss their difficulties. As one of my pupils said to me, "I got no problems. The only problem I got is I'm thinking of running away from home." Play therapy, aside from being cathartic, is a way to reveal the child's inner world, his difficulties and conflicts. Imagery can be seen as a unique form of play therapy, but imagery goes a step further because it guides the child to find his own solutions, and enables him to do that which in his conscious life he has not yet attempted. Having solved a problem by means of imagery, he is subsequently able to translate the solution into his real life. He will have found a way to go where he has not yet been, to try something new or different, to move from a position of feeling stuck or controlled. He is now open to experience possibilities previously not contemplated.

Children, by and large, have a hard time concentrating for any length of time. However, you have only to mention the word "game" or to present something in the form of a game and all this changes. I've observed a fourteen-year-old girl who was mentally challenged concentrate on games for four hours without getting distracted or even briefly losing attention. The tasks she was learning were done in the form of a game, and she reveled in it. Imagery, too, is a form of game and can engage children for long periods of time.

Children also like to do things by themselves. We've all seen adults trying to feed toddlers who grab the spoon away and utter, "Me do it, me do it." In imagery, we don't do anything for children—we merely guide them to do by themselves what they want to achieve. This gives them a sense of power, accomplishment, autonomy, and success. In place of helplessness and lack of control or even frustration and despair, we put independence and confidence, motivation and hope.

Imagination plays a constant part in the life of a child. One has only to watch little children at play to see how rich, vivid, and alive their imaginative world is. With the most meager of toys, children construct farms and cities, beaches and battlegrounds, heroes and rascals. They give each of their dolls names and characters and place them in locations such as hospitals, schools, and families. Even without toys, young children will take boxes or cartons and chairs, specifically arrange them, and imagine they are in a train, at sea, in an airplane, or exploring space. Imagery plays right into the natural creativity and resourcefulness of children.

Imagery is a perfect way to work with children. It appeals to their natural ability to imagine and to their sense of fun. Because it is done in the form of a game, it opens them up to reveal what they might otherwise feel inhibited or bashful about or what they might be unable to express verbally.

Imagery helps children easily solve little problems. By solving these everyday problems, they learn to deal with difficulties and become confident that difficulties are to be surmounted, be they emotional, behavioral, or physical. In this manner, they become freer and less frightened. When a child uses imagery to find solutions to problems in her current life or from the past, she obtains a sense of autonomy and confidence in her ability to resolve situations she may have felt controlled her. These situations run the gamut of the child's experience, pertaining to her relationship with herself, her peers, her parents, siblings, teachers, authority figures, and learning situations in school, to name a few. Using imagination to find solutions to these situations has the added advantage of improving the child's verbal ability, because the images are clear and precise, and they lend themselves to clarity and precision of expression.

Through imagery, the parent or teacher gets to see the inner world of the child: how she feels about herself, what she feels towards her siblings, whether she has an inferiority or superiority complex, if she is a loner, whether she gets easily frustrated and quits, how her friends see her, whether she feels helpless or autonomous, and whether she is a victim or able to impact her environment. These and other aspects of the child's psychological makeup, which may be hidden from her parents and teachers, often come to light through imagery. The child does not feel attacked, interrogated, or pried into, but sees the exercises as a game of imagination. Consequently, she does not feel the need to be defensive. Thus the adults working with the child, and the child herself, will gain valuable insights and important information leading to clearer awareness. The parent or teacher will then know how to deal with the child in a way that will be positive and empowering. Instead of exacerbating problems due to lack of knowledge, parents and teachers who work with imagery are in a position to ameliorate situations. For example, a child who sees no colors or consistently sees only black or gray may be depressed. The parent or teacher can, by observation, determine if this is the case or not. Should the depression be verified, they can take the necessary steps to help the child. Similarly, if it becomes apparent that the child has many fears, lacks self-worth, or is hostile or aggressive to an exaggerated degree, appropriate measures can be taken once parents and teachers are aware of this. Sometimes, what is called for are follow-up exercises geared towards a specific goal. For example, when a child feels stuck, exercises opening doors and windows may be helpful.

Finally, it is important to recognize that imagery is quite different from fantasy. The latter takes the child away from dealing concretely with her difficulties into a world of escape and unreality. Imagery, on the other hand, teaches the child to deal concretely with her everyday difficulties, relying on her own inner knowledge, wisdom, and resources.

How to Use this Book

When we do imagery exercises with children, we are able to see and get them to see what their issues are. Imagery highlights their typical responses and enables us to see what their patterns and habits are. With this knowledge, we are able to guide them towards change, suggesting alternative ways of responding or letting them find new paths as yet untried by them. It is expecting too much from a young child for him to change in one session, although this does sometimes happen. We do not have to ask children to change themselves but rather to change their environment into something less acute, less difficult, less aggressive. Children have a natural tendency to do this.

Each of the book's six chapters contains several groups of thematic guided imagery exercises, which I have designed to make the topics relevant, interesting, and practical. These exercises draw upon the imagination of the child and will guide him towards a deeper understanding of himself, helping him get in touch with his own inner knowing and intuitive self. Generally, results from an imagery exercise can be achieved in a week by doing the exercise daily for several consecutive days. To consolidate the effect, the exercise should be done for two more weeks in a row.

While the exercises are numbered, this does not mean that the guide must give them to the children in that specific order—the numbering distinguishes exercises from one another, and provides an easy reference point for the reader.

I advise you not to overload the child with too many exercises at once. Very few exercises should be given at any one time, preferably only one at a time, so as to avoid the mingling of images and to permit the experience to continue to work in the unconscious mind. However, where the exercise develops in a series of images, then all facets of that exercise can be given in one sitting. In addition, when children are seen only once a week, you can give them more than one exercise so they have one for each day. It is however preferable that they stay with one exercise for the duration of a week.

It is important to do the exercises quickly, taking no more than two minutes at first. With practice, you can reduce the time to one minute per exercise. Keeping the exercises short avoids the tendency of children to daydream.

I wrote this book with the intention of making children become competent people who are able to direct their lives in the way they want. It is a book that takes children on a trip to discover themselves—but it does not stop there. Should they so wish, the children can keep a notebook in which they record their experiences of the exercises and draw what they see. On the first page, they may want to put on the left side the things they want to change in themselves and on the right side the things they want to obtain or develop.

A good way to work with this book is to proceed weekly, focusing the children on one thing they wish to change and one thing they wish to develop. If a detrimental habit has been with them for a long time, it may take a program of three weeks to change it.

Finally, you can do this work individually, with one child at a time, or in a small group setting or even with an entire class. Children can also do it with a friend. I recommend that you, the adult, try some of these exercises yourself to get a sense of how they work. You can make a tape of the exercises and play them back to yourself. But again, try only two or three exercises at one time. For yourself, or the children with whom you work, if there is one exercise that is especially pleasing, stay with that one. You may pick a different series at another time, depending on what area of life you are working on and in which realm you wish to see results.

Three-Week Calendar Cycle

I recommend doing the exercises for three weeks and then taking one week off to rest. This cycle enables the child to register the new teaching so it becomes ingrained in her body. In this way she creates a new habit. The week off gives the body a chance to continue the work by itself, which happens because many images have an emotional energy of their own. If the intention is to change a habit that has been present for a long time, I recommend repeating the three-week cycle after resting for one week.

Administering the Exercises: General Instructions

At the start of each exercise, begin with the following induction:

"Sit comfortably in a chair with your legs uncrossed. Your hands should be resting on your knees, palms up." *Note to Guide: This enables the energy to flow freely in the body.* "Close your eyes and keep them closed until I tell you to open them. This helps us see things that we can't see with our eyes open. We will keep our eyes closed no more than two minutes. Now breathe out slowly through your mouth three times. Let me hear the sound of your breath coming out of your mouth as you slowly release the air." *Note to Guide: Pause a couple of seconds to let the child finish breathing out; then begin the exercise. Throughout the exercise, feel free to pause for no more than a couple of seconds as necessary, then continue on. At the end of the exercise, pause very briefly and then say, "Breathe out and open your eyes."*

Breathing out has the effect of quieting all of their internal organs. It also relaxes the children, which enables the images to readily come up. Where an exercise is long, they may want to breathe out during it to rest a little. It is advisable to cut a long exercise in parts when it is difficult to do it in a very short time. When you end the exercise, tell the children to breathe out one time before opening their eyes. In the rare situation that a child feels great discomfort during an exercise, do not continue with the exercise but tell him to open his eyes and take a break.

When the exercise is over, have the children open their eyes and tell or write about what they saw, how they felt, and what happened. You may want to ask the children what they learned about themselves, someone else, or about life. Have them relate their experience in the present tense, for example, "I see" rather than "I saw"; "It is blue," rather than "It was blue." Use of the present tense keeps the image active and alive. After they verbally share their experiences, I often invite the children to draw pictures of what they saw, using the colors that they saw in their imagery. I also suggest that they write about it using prose or poetry.

Finally, when listening to their responses, it is best not to interrupt and of utmost importance to avoid judging a response or giving advice. By refraining from these actions, we respect the child and his experiences and not only validate him, but encourage his confidence and trust, and strengthen his intuition.

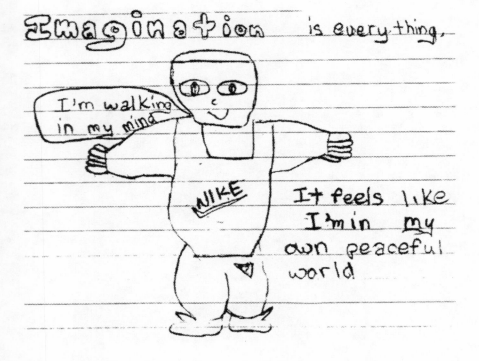

CHAPTER

1

Discovering the Self

"I love guided imagery because it helps me express myself, and makes me get all that I want out, and it lets me see my own self. It makes me feel like a whole new person."

—Gilbert, age 9

Who Are You?

Many have said there is no greater knowledge than knowledge of oneself. Most people are oblivious to themselves, while others know only certain aspects of their personalities. Remaining in a state of darkness about ourselves keeps us stuck, thereby preventing progress. Change is only possible where there is an element of awareness present. Defenses have to be worked through, so that we can picture ourselves as we really are. Only then is it possible to make the decision to transform. When this happens, we are no longer ruled by circumstances, but we become rulers of our circumstances. Clearly, this not only changes, but also enriches the quality of our personalities and of our lives.

The following section provides exercises that can be done with children to enable them to better understand themselves and find out more about their likes and dislikes.

At the start of each exercise, begin with the following induction:

"Sit comfortably in a chair with your legs uncrossed. Your hands should be resting on your knees, palms up. Close your eyes and keep them closed until I tell you to open them. This helps us see things that we can't see with our eyes open. We will keep our eyes closed no more than two minutes. Now breathe out slowly through your mouth three times. Let me hear the sound of your breath coming out of your mouth as you slowly release the air."

> *Note to Guide: Pause a couple of seconds to let the child finish breathing out, then begin the exercise. At the end of the exercise, pause very briefly, then say, "Breathe out once and open your eyes."*

Sample Exercise

You have in your hand a dictionary.
Open this dictionary.
Select all the words that describe you as you now are.
What are those words?
Now choose and write down in your imagination
All the words that describe how you would like to be.
What are these words?
See yourself acting as if you had these qualities or traits now.

> *Note to Guide: Pause a few seconds, then continue.)*
> *Breathe out once and open your eyes.*

Child's Response

The words could talk, they pop out, they read and dance. I can hear them singing. They have colors. The colors are red, blue, green, purple, yellow, brown, and orange. I see a lot of words. I hear them sing: "I feel you feel happy, sad. Angry and mad. We feel happy, sad. Very angry and very mad."

In my dictionary I see the good things about myself. I have friends,

I'm nice, I do homework, I am neat and I clean up.

The bad things are I get in trouble and I make noise.

—Jacqueline, age 8

The following exercises will help children to explore and learn more about themselves:

Exercise 1
Imagine you are an eagle.
How does it feel to be an eagle?
Now be a tiny little hummingbird.
Which do you like better and why?

Exercise 2
Imagine you are a peacock
Strutting proudly in the park.
As you open your tail of many colors
And hear everyone praise your beauty.
Tell how you feel being the peacock.

The next set of exercises will help children come to know themselves better and will also help them take the necessary and appropriate action in any given situation. To take action, children must know what they want. The last exercise will help children relax.

Exercise 3
See the letter A.
See yourself as the letter A in the alphabet.
How does it feel to be A?
See the letter Z.

Now see yourself as the letter Z in the alphabet.

How does it feel to be Z?

Exercise 4

See yourself in a place you would like to be more than any other
  place.

Where is this place?

What are you doing?

Who is there with you?

And what is happening?

Exercise 5

See yourself doing something you are frightened of.

Have someone you like or who likes you (someone supportive)
  with you.

What are you doing?

And how are you doing it?

And what is happening?

Exercise 6

Imagine a place where you feel perfectly calm and at ease.

Describe this place.

Put yourself in this place and sense feeling calm, happy, and safe.

Invite someone you like, or some people you like, into this place.

Tell what is happening.

How do you feel with the person you have invited?

Exercise 7

You have in your hand a can opener

Which will open up any part of yourself

That you feel or know needs to be open.

You begin to use it

And open up first one, then another part of yourself.

What parts are you opening?

How are you behaving and feeling now that these parts are open?

Breathe out.

Are there any parts that you do not wish to open yet?

Identify what they are.

Be aware of the reason you do not wish to open them now.

Child's Respons

I like being the letter "A." It is fun being the letter "A" because I am the first letter in the alphabet. I love being a leader. I am important because without me the alphabet will not be the alphabet!

The only thing I don't like about being the first letter is the way I look. "A" does not have a face, hands or feet. "A" is not a living thing. That is why I'd rather be a person than a letter.

I hate being the letter "Z" because it is the last letter in the alphabet and has to wait a long time for its turn to come around.

—George, age 11

How Do You Feel about Yourself in Relationship to Others?

"It doesn't matter how tall or how short you are on the outside, it matters how you feel on the inside."

—Andrew, age 8

Knowing yourself is not sufficient. We all have to learn how to relate to the people around us. The following exercises are designed to bring awareness to the nature of interpersonal relations. This section will help children get along better with themselves and others. They will also learn to appreciate similarities and differences in people, which will make them more tolerant of each other.

Giant and Dwarf Series

Exercise 8
Be a giant in a land of giants.
How is it to be a giant in this land?

Exercise 9
Be a giant in a land of dwarfs.
How is it to be a giant in this land?

Exercise 10
Be a dwarf in a land of dwarfs.

Do you like it?

What are you doing?

What is everyone else doing?

> I would like to be giant because I can pick any body up. even a big wrestler. it would make me feel strong and proud.
>
> I would also like to be a dwarf because if I tried to get in someplace they wouldn't see me.
>
> Monique
> 8 years old

Exercise 11

Be a dwarf in a land of giants.

What is happening?

How are you feeling?

Child's Response

I closed my eyes, and I imagined I was a giant. It was a little bit scary because when people saw you they would run away, and when you walk, you would break the houses or buildings. And it would be sad because you would have no one to talk to.

Being a dwarf would be fun because you could hide in certain places, and if a giant tries to step on you, you could run under his legs and make him fall. It would be great to be a dwarf.

From this I learned that if you are different, like from a different country or something, some people would not like you.

—Susan, age 10

Mountain Series

Exercise 12

Be the tallest mountain talking to the smallest mountain.
What are you saying?

Exercise 13

Be the smallest mountain talking to the tallest mountain.
What are you saying?
What are you feeling?

Exercise 14

Be a medium-sized mountain.
Say something to the smallest mountain.
Hear it say something back to you.

Exercise 15

Be a medium-sized mountain.
Say something to the tallest mountain.
What are you saying?
What is it saying back to you?

Exercise 16

Be a medium-sized mountain.

Say something to another medium-sized mountain.

What are you saying?

What is it saying to you?

Which mountain do you prefer to be and why?

Exercise 17

See yourself standing at the foot of a mountain.

How big is your mountain?

Now be standing at the top of the mountain.

How does it feel to be at the foot of this mountain?

How does it feel to be at the top?

Child's Response

Being the tallest mountain is not all it's pictured to be. It's one thing to want to be unique and look your own way, but when you're the tallest, you feel you're not normal. The other mountains may tease you, and even though you attract more tourists, your own people (the mountains) treat you as an outcast.

Being the smallest mountain is not much different, because you're still an outcast. Most mountains, like people, will tease you if you are not what they expect or normal.

—Chantal, age 13

Chantal's response is both interesting and revealing, and quite different from Andrew's at the beginning of this section. Imagery is great for bringing out the uniqueness of each child. Here we see how Chantal feels about social relationships. Her concern to be accepted by her peers supersedes all other concerns. Though intellectually gifted and capable of coming out ahead of everyone, she chooses not to do so because more than anything she wants to be one of the crowd at this point in her life. This is normal for teenagers and is often referred to as the "herd instinct."

Planet Series

Note to Guide: Make the following exercise very short and ask the children to return to their own conscious place before they tell what has happened. This is necessary because some children find it hard to come back to the here and now.

Exercise 18

See yourself as the sun.

How is it to be the sun?

Do you like it?

Tell why or why not.

It is great to be the sun. You get to make people happy and make plants grow. You can make the plants grow by shining on them. You can make the people wear shorts and make a bad weather good

Exercise 19

See yourself as the moon.

How is it to be the moon?

Do you like it?

Which do you prefer to be, the sun or the moon?

Which do you prefer to be — the sun or the mo[on]
The moon because I think people mostly look at the moon
because I people are always in a rush and they don't
realy look at the sun so but when it is so dark
you can't help but look at the moon.

Exercise 20

Have the sun say something to the moon.

And have the moon say something to the sun.

What is each saying?

Exercise 21

See yourself as a star.

How is it to be a star?

If you know the star that was above the earth

At the time of your birth, become this star.

Exercise 22

Now be the planet earth.

Tell how it is to be the planet earth.

Exercise 23

See and hear yourself as a star

Saying something to yourself as the earth.

And have the earth say something to the star.

What is each saying?

Exercise 24

See where in your body is your sun.

Breathe out.

And see where in your body is your moon.

Breathe out.

Now tell where in your body is your star.

Exercise 25

See and sense in your body where the four elements are.

Where do you sense the water in your body?

Where do you sense the air in your body?

Where do you sense the fire in your body?

And where do you sense the earth in your body?

Children's Responses

It feels good to be the sun because I can give light to people.
And sometimes I can dry clothes. I am bigger than everyone else,
and they do look up to me. It makes me feel happy. I am big and
powerful, and I don't like being alone.

I could be powerful if I could rule my own life. I mean like making my own decisions, as in what to wear, how to comb my hair, when to see the dentist, and what kind of friends I should have. I want the kind of friend who tells the truth—not the kind of friend who gives you advice to hurt you.

—Cindy, age 11

Being the sun, I will shine for people who have frozen food, if they want to unfreeze it. Except for ice cream. I feel like a king, like I have some kind of power to give people what they want. That's it.

—Melissa, age 11

The Planet Series leads naturally into the subject of creation. Before doing the Garden of Eden exercises, I'd like to refresh you on the story as told in the Bible. In the beginning, God created the world. And in this world He put a most wondrous garden, the Garden of Eden. Every tree that God had created was in this garden. So, too, every animal, or bird, or creepy crawly was in the garden. Finally, God created Adam and Eve, the first two people ever to be created. He put them in the beautiful garden too. Then God said to Adam, "From all the trees of the garden, you may eat. But," said God, "there is one exception: the Tree of Knowledge. From this tree you may not eat."

Along came the serpent and said to Eve, "Look how beautiful the fruit of this tree is." As you guessed, it was the Tree of Knowledge about which the serpent spoke. Then the serpent convinced Eve to eat of the forbidden fruit. Eve saw that it tasted good, and she gave it to Adam so that he might eat of it too. And Adam ate it.

Then God said, "Where are you, Adam, and where are you, Eve?"

13

But they were too frightened to answer. Then God continued, "For the sin of having eaten of the forbidden fruit, you can no longer stay in this beautiful garden. But instead you must go out into the world and work hard for your keep."

So it was that Adam and Eve were sent out of the garden, and the serpent was punished by having to grovel in the earth for its food.

I have chosen to include the story of the Garden of Eden in this book, because it is an archetypal story. The themes apply equally well to all societies, all cultures, and all times. I see in this story many possibilities for developing a child's character because the themes it deals with are ones which children encounter on a daily basis, such as the temptation to sin or disobey authority. The story also teaches the importance of personal responsibility, and brings awareness that there are consequences for actions and choices. These exercises also show children the need to distinguish between true friends and those who purport to be their friends.

The Garden of Eden Series

Exercise 26
Breathe out.
Be any tree you like in the Garden of Eden.
Which tree are you?
Describe what it is like to be this tree.

Exercise 27
Now be the Tree of Knowledge, knowing Good and Evil.
How is it to have this knowledge?
What do you know that you didn't know before?
And what do you do that you didn't do before?

Exercise 28

See a screen.

On the screen you see

Adam, Eve,

The Forbidden Fruit,

And the snake.

See them in the same moment all together.

What is happening?

Exercise 29

See the Tree of Knowledge returning slowly to the seed.

See and sense what is happening.

Exercise 30

Be a seed.

Tell what seed you are.

Describe what it feels like.

Do you sense the great energy

That being the seed is giving you?

See and tell what you would like to do with this extra energy.

Exercise 31

Imagine you are the snake in the Garden of Eden.

How do you feel as this snake?

Tell what you are doing

And what is happening.

Children's Responses

I would both like to be that tree and not like to be it. I would like
to be the Tree of Knowledge because I would be smarter than

anyone in the world. But then again I would not like to be the
Tree of Knowledge because I would know all of the bad things
that will happen in the future. And I would like to discover things
like a normal person, and these are my feelings about the Tree of
Knowledge.

—Samantha, age 11

It's kind of fun being the Tree of Knowledge because everyone
comes to you with their problems and questions, and they look up
to you for the answer. It makes me feel wanted, known, special.
It makes me feel good about myself, especially when they tell me
something personal about themselves, and know that I would never
tell a soul about it.

On the other hand, it can be kind of frustrating. Maybe at least one
day out of the year you could get some peace and quiet. But no,
everyone wants to know what you think. It's flattering, but you just
get sick of it sometimes. The Tree of Knowledge has problems of
its own, too, you know.

Maybe others wouldn't think of me so highly. They may think I am
a show-off or that I think I am better than everyone else. All I want
to do is help others in need, that's all.

—Tyler, age 14

The Withdrawn Child
Some children withdraw from the world around them. These
withdrawn children often get neglected because it is the noisy
child who tends to get attention. It is important to help withdrawn
children come out of their shell, but one must do this delicately,
and with respect for the child. Imagery is a good way to help the

withdrawn child because the child will not open up any more than
he is ready to and, therefore, will not get hurt.

Exercise 32

Be a snail in the garden hiding inside your shell.
Find something that makes you come out
And tell what it is.
How do you feel, having come out?

Exercise 33

Be a little but beautiful flower
Hidden under a bush.
What is this flower feeling?
Why is it hiding under the bush?

Exercise 34

Imagine you are an express train that stays in the train shed
And goes nowhere.
What is happening and how do you feel?

Exercise 35

Imagine a flute that no one plays,
So the music is not coming out.
Tell how the flute feels.

Exercise 36

Imagine a gift that stays unopened,
Wrapped up beautifully,
But hidden inside the box.

Tell how the gift feels.

Tell how the person who gave the gift feels.

Exercise 37

Imagine a house that no one lives in.

How does the house feel?

How can the house get people to visit?

Or better still, to live in it?

Exercise 38

See a zipper down your chest.

Now slowly open the zipper

And sense what is happening in your body.

Now close this zipper

And sense again what is happening to your body.

What sensations and feelings do you have

When you open the zipper,

And when you close the zipper?

Exercise 39

Be a caterpillar turning into a butterfly

Describe what is happening as you stretch your wings.

The next exercise is for children who don't talk for one reason or another, children who are introverted, or children who are very secretive and don't speak to their family or their teachers, so we have to give them a way to help themselves.

This exercise can be done during the course of one trimester. Every day the child keeps adding to it as things come up in her life. The exercise is done physically, with paper and colored pencils or crayons. Through the child drawing on the paper, the form of pain is externalized from the body, which helps her deal with her difficulties. For this exercise you will need paper, crayons, or colored pencils. Try to provide many colors for the child to choose from. This will help you determine which colors the child prefers.

Exercise: The Flower

Have the child begin by drawing a circle on a large sheet of paper. Tell the child that this circle is herself. Instruct the child to draw petals at the top of the circle, which will represent things that she loves or likes or are interesting to her. The petals can be in every color. Tell her the petals can be her mother, another relative, a friend, or a pet.

Next, have the child add petals all around the top of the circle, as many things or people as she finds interesting to her.

At the right side of the circle have her put petals that represent what she wants or wishes for herself. Examples include friends or goals or other things the child desires.

At the bottom, have the child put petals for things she hates or that discourage her, for things that don't permit her to be free and stop her from growing. She can feel free to put actual words in the petals.

Now at the left, have the child put petals that represent people or events that have given her trouble in the past and that still affect her life.

You can extend this exercise with the following additional drawing:

Have the child color the petals at the bottom of the page with a color she dislikes, which will symbolize the things she hates. After she does this, have her color over those petals with colors she likes. She should use pastel colors, if possible, to cover the petals and the words. This will help these painful petals to fall away and disappear from her life.

Actually, the things from her life don't disappear, but take on a different meaning as she learns to turn these painful events into lessons from which to learn. As the child overcomes these difficulties, she will become stronger. And she will keep adding to the left side because every yesterday is part of the past.

The following exercises will help the child bring inner thoughts and feelings out into consciousness. When this happens, the feelings can be talked about and put into proper perspective. The trick is to get the children to talk.

Exercise 40
Be a hermit and close yourself in a cave to study.
When you are ready, come out of your cave,
Holding a light in your hand.
Tell what you see, know, and feel.
What did you learn when in the cave?

Exercise 41
Imagine you are a toy car that needs to be wound up to go.
Tell how it feels and who is winding you up.

Exercise 42
Imagine you are in a garden surrounded by a little wall.
If you can knock down that wall,
There are many treasures for you in the garden.

Tell how you are doing it.

What do you learn about yourself?

What treasures do you find?

Exercise 43

Beyond the wall are all the toys or games that you like.

Do you prefer to climb over the wall,

Or to knock the wall down?

Tell why.

Self-Esteem

"Before I came to you, I felt like a worm. Now I feel like a giant."

—Jessica, age 8

The meaning of self-esteem is how you value yourself. So many of us are proud when we should be humble and humble when we should be proud. We have no real concept of our true value. This generally reflects the way we have been treated by significant others in our formative years.

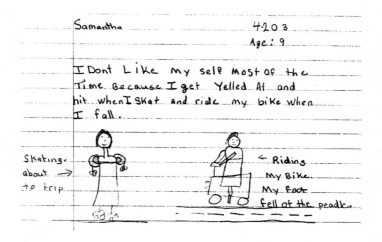

Often we value ourselves quite differently from the way others perceive us. We might still be ridden with shame and guilt, emotions which prevent us from seeing and feeling our true worth.

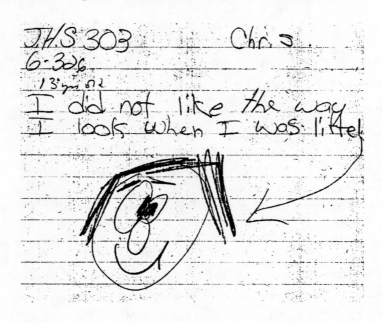

JHS 303   Chris

6-306

13 yrs old

I did not like the way I looks when I was little

Others, meanwhile, see our talents, our gifts, and how special we are. We see ourselves in a fragmented manner; we may perceive ourselves as able in one area of our life but inadequate in other areas. For example, I might see myself as a capable teacher, yet in the social arena, I may feel incompetent. The ideal is to aim for an integrated personality.

I am stupid becous I made a mistake.

Julius 3-10 9

Age 8

The following exercises will help children feel good about themselves, appreciate themselves, and feel worthy without becoming arrogant.

Exercice 44
See a time you helped somebody
With something they couldn't do.
And notice how you succeeded.
Tell what you did and also how you felt.

Exercise 45
See yourself working out a puzzle
That you thought you could never do.
Notice that every time you want to give up,
A little voice inside you says, "Keep on"
Until the puzzle is finished
And you feel so proud.
Tell about this proud feeling.

Exercise 46
A new child comes to your class.
He feels totally bewildered.
Nobody is helping him,
So you go and help him.
Now you see how happy he is.
And now you see how happy you are.
Tell about these happy feelings.

Exercise 47
See yourself trying to ride a bike,

But you find it very difficult.

You tell yourself, "Keep trying, keep trying,

I'll be so proud if I can ride my bike."

You keep trying until you succeed.

Notice how proud you are because you did it all yourself.

Tell about this proud feeling.

Exercise 48

See yourself not knowing how to do some things

You once knew how to do.

Sense how stupid and foolish you feel.

You tell yourself,

"If I could do those things once,

I can do them again,

Provided I really work at it."

Suddenly you find you have succeeded.

You feel like a hero.

Tell what some of those things are you can now do.

Exercise 49

You are one of the colors of a rainbow.

What color are you?

Where in the rainbow are you?

Move around to be in different positions

And see how it feels.

Exercise 50

You are the hero or heroine in a play.

Tell what is happening,

And how it feels to be the hero or heroine.

Exercise 51

Imagine you are in a wide-open space,

Where lots of green plants are growing.

See that each plant is different from the others.

Notice each is its own shade of green,

Its own form, its own size.

Notice that each has its own space

And all are beautiful.

See, and know that you are one of these beautiful green plants.

Making Consistent Efforts Towards Goals

Children need to learn to do things in a consistent and persistent manner in order to attain a desired goal. They also need to know that there are many methods they can use to reach the same goal. The exercises that follow will help children attain self-reliance and learn whom they can trust. Pay attention to see if the child likes to control the situation. If so, the exercises may help him understand why he has the feeling that he must do it all by himself and ask for help only as a last resort. See whether these exercises bring back memories such as, "The day I felt I was grown up was the day I could stand up on the swings."

Exercise 52

See yourself sitting on a swing in a park.

You can't seem to make the swing go up high.

What are you doing?

How are you feeling?

What is happening?

Do you ask someone to push you

Or push off with your feet against the ground?

Do you push off with your upper arms
Or stand up and push off with your upper arms and legs?
Or do you do something else you think will work?
Which way do you like the best and for what reason?

Exercise 53
You try to open a bottle, but the lid is very tight.
What are you doing?
How do you succeed in opening it?

Exercise 54
You are in a stuffy room.
You go to the window to open it, but it is stuck.
What is happening?

Exercise 55
There is a present for you.
But it is high up in a tree.
How do you get it down?
Can you see how if you want something badly,
You easily find the way to have it?
Can you apply this to getting a good grade in school?

Inner Resources

We all have inner resources, but sometimes, because we have
developed bad habits, such as dependency, feelings of helplessness,
or self-doubt, we remain oblivious to them. Inner resources can
be identified and developed through use. These exercises will help
children discover resources they never knew they possessed.

Exercise 56

See yourself in a rowboat.

Describe the exact place where you are.

Describe the scenery.

Tell if anyone is there with you.

Tell how you feel being in this rowboat

And where you arrive in it.

Exercise 57

See yourself in a sailboat.

Describe the scenery.

Tell if you are with someone or alone.

How do you like being in this sailboat?

And where do you arrive?

Exercise 58

You are now in a motorboat.

Tell what it is like to be in this motorboat.

Is anyone there with you?

Where does this motorboat take you?

Which of the boats do you like being in best?

Exercise 59

See yourself in a maze.

What kind of maze is it?

Describe what is happening.

What are you feeling?

How do you get out?

Exercise 60

You are walking in the park on the grass.

Suddenly you feel yourself sinking in a bog.
With each step you take you are sinking deeper.
What is happening?

Exercise 61
You are walking on a clearly marked path in the forest.
Suddenly the trail disappears.
What do you feel?
What do you do?

Exercise 62
You are rowing in a lake
When far out from the shore,
You notice the boat is leaking water.
What do you do?

Exercise 63
You are rowing in a lake
And lose one oar.
What do you do?

Exercise 64
You are the queen bee
In a hive of hundreds of bees.
Tell what is happening.
How do you like it?

Exercise 65
You are a drone bee.
You work very hard.

Tell what you are doing.
How do you like it?

Exercise 66

You are the honey
That the bees are making.
What is happening to you?
What feelings do you have?

The following exercises will enhance the ability of children to be resourceful in challenging situations. As they learn to find solutions to the imaginary difficulties in these exercises, they will also be learning how to resolve difficulties in their lives.

Exercise 67

Picture yourself lost in a fog.
You can hardly see what's in front of you.
How do you feel?
What do you do?

Exercise 68

You are locked in a room.
You have a box containing many keys.
How do you find the right one?

Exercise 69

You are cooking your favorite meal
But you have very few ingredients.
How are you managing to cook the meal?

Exercise 70

You cook something you like,
But you put too much salt in.
How are you correcting it?
Does it work?

Exercise 71

A new girl comes to your class
Who doesn't speak your language.
You want to communicate something.
How are you doing it?

Exercise 72

You are crossing a suspension bridge.
It is a windy day.
The bridge is swaying.
How are you maintaining your balance?

Exercise 73

You have been to the beach
And have lost one shoe.
Do you prefer to walk with one shoe on and one shoe off
Or with no shoes?
What is the reason?

Exercise 74

You are walking with very thin shoes
Over a very rocky path.
You feel every stone under your feet.
What are you doing?

Exercise 75

You are walking barefoot

Over a very rocky path.

What is happening?

Do You Love Yourself?
Sharing Your Heart with Yourself and Others

In Western civilizations, some people find it very hard to express
their feelings. This can stultify their growth and their ability to
relate to others. The following exercises will help children get in
touch with their inner feelings.

Exercise 76

See yourself looking at a picture of your heart.

> *Note to Guide: You may want to show them an actual
> picture.*

Know that this heart is your faithful servant,

Beating ceaselessly, day in, day out, year in, year out.

See and hear yourself giving thanks to your heart

For keeping you alive.

Exercise 77

Put your hands on your heart

And feel the rhythm of its beat.

Sense how calm you are

When in touch with your own rhythmic heartbeat.

Sense your heart pumping blood

To every part of your body,

Bringing oxygen to each cell and renewing it.

Sense this new moment-by-moment life
In every cell of your body.

Exercise 78
With your hands on your heart,
Decide how you wish to share your heart with yourself today.
What are you doing to share your heart with yourself?
Are you encouraging yourself to do those things that help you
   succeed?
What are some of those things?

Exercise 79
See how you are sharing your heart with people around you.
Whom do you share your heart with?
And how are you doing it?
See and sense what is happening when you share your heart with
   others.

Exercise 80
How do you feel when you share your heart with yourself and
   others?
Are there any people you do not wish to share your heart with?
What is the reason for this?

Exercise 81
Who are the people you wish would share their heart with you?
See them doing this now.
What is happening and what are you feeling?

Exercise: Loving Yourself

Jimmy, age 12, was referred to me because his work wasn't up to par. Instead of paying attention in class, he would fool around and seemed to enjoy being the class clown. When he walked into my room I got a sense of a sad boy who had given up. Rather than let anyone see how sad he was, he spent his time and energy making everyone laugh.

"Jimmy," I said, "sometimes we act one way on the outside but feel quite different on the inside. I have a feeling that might be happening with you. What do you say?"

"I don't know."

"Would you like to find out?"

"Okay. But how will I find out?"

"Sometimes when we close our eyes we can take a look at what's inside us. Are you ready to try?"

"Yes, I'm ready," said Jimmy.

"Good. If at any time you don't like what you see, simply open your eyes."

Counselor: Close your eyes. Breathe out through your mouth slowly three times. Feel nice and relaxed and imagine yourself getting smaller so you can enter your heart. See yourself inside your heart exploring. Tell me what you see.

Jimmy: I see blue, a blue dot. It's right in the center of the heart. It's a dark blue.

Counselor: Ask the blue what it means and why it's there. What does it say?

Jimmy: It says the blue dot is there when the heart is sad; it gets larger when it's very angry.

Counselor: Ask it to give you some examples of when it gets larger.

Jimmy: It says when it's made fun of. When it's yelled at. When it often doesn't get what it wants.

Counselor: Like what?

Jimmy: Like happiness.

Counselor: How do you feel being in the heart?

Jimmy: I feel happy because all that is in the heart is love and joy.

Counselor: Your heart wants to give you a piece of advice. Imagine you have a stethoscope and listen carefully to what the heart is telling you. Do you hear?

Jimmy: Yes! Yes! The heart says it wants to get rid of the blue spot. It says all I have to do is be happy as much as I can and that will make the heart be happy.

Counselor: It's not that easy to be happy, is it?

Jimmy: The heart says Christmas is coming soon and I hope you get something you want and that will make you happy and then the blue spot will go away.

Counselor: How do you feel now, Jimmy?

Jimmy: I feel relaxed but sorry for my heart.

Counselor: Put your hands on your heart and give it lots of love. Tell it you will always love it no matter what. Even if people yell at you, or make fun of you, you will imagine you are wearing a coat of armor so those words cannot penetrate.

Jimmy: Spontaneously, "the blue spot got smaller."

I am giveing Love and Joy to my hart.

Follow-up Exercise: Looking for the Pain

Counselor: Imagine you're traveling in your body, you have a little lamp and you're looking for where your pain is. Where in your body is your pain?

Jimmy: In my mind.

Counselor: Where in your mind?

Jimmy: It's the part of the mind that makes you feel things, not physical but mentally. Like if you're sad and you don't tell anyone. If you keep it inside, then you're feeling it mentally, not physically.

Counselor: And how does that feel?

Jimmy: It's like a pain in your head that's telling you whatever you feel in your head that's making you feel that pain is wrong.

Counselor: How does the pain look?

Jimmy: It's a big blue light.

Counselor: Ask it how long it's been there.

Jimmy: A year.

Counselor: Ask it if something happened that created this pain.

Jimmy: It tells me something that I shouldn't be doing.

Counselor: Like what?

Jimmy: Like I should know more of what's right, to be more serious.

Counselor: Can you explain that a little better?

Jimmy: It thinks I play too much.

Counselor: So see a scale. On one side is how much you play and on the other side is how serious you are. Do you see it?

Jimmy: Yes.

Counselor: Okay, very good, so tell me what you see.

Jimmy: The play is heavier.

Counselor: See if you can see more precisely how much heavier?

Jimmy: The serious is thirty per cent, and the play is seventy per cent.

Counselor: Now see the perfect scale that would take away the sad feeling.

Jimmy: If the play and the serious were balanced fifty-fifty.

Counselor: Know that you have a very good brain and that you know all the answers. Find the part that knows everything.

Jimmy: I found it! It's far away. It's very far from the part that's sad, in my mind.

Counselor: Ask the part that knows everything how you can balance your scale, what you need to do.

Jimmy: When it's time for me to be serious, I have to pay more attention to what I'm doing, and when it's time for me to play, I have to play more seriously.

Counselor: Great. So now balance your scale so that it's fifty-fifty. Do you see it?

Jimmy: Yes I see it.

Counselor: How do you feel?

Jimmy: The blue light disappeared.

Counselor: Anything else come in its place?

Jimmy: A red light, a deep red. The red light represents LOVE.

Counselor: Very nice. So when you're in balance you feel love. Wonderful! You really are a loving person. Now whom do you want to give this love to?

Jimmy: To all people I care about.

Counselor: Wonderful, and remember to give some to yourself.

CHAPTER

2
Connecting With Others

*"My day after imaging is usually better. I get
in less fights now. It kind of feels like predicting
the future. Try imaging each morning and plan
your day. Just try it for 30 days, I guarantee it
will work."*

—Patrick, age 11

I love My family so so so much
they are a best family,

Getting Along with Siblings

Learning how to behave with older and younger siblings in a way
that is fair and just can be a hard but important lesson to learn.
How children interact with their siblings and the feelings generated

in these interactions will determine to some extent how they will relate to people and groups at large later on in life. Does the child assume a protective role of others, or does he feel the need to protect himself from others? Does he vie for attention, or does he give attention? Is he argumentative or peace loving? Does he act out of anger or the need for approval? These and other attitudes and behavior patterns are formed early on in life, learned in our earliest interactions within the family framework. Often these patterns stay with us into adulthood, especially in the absence of awareness and intervention. Do we feel anger, or do we act out of the need for approval? The following exercises are designed to deepen the child's understanding of his own feelings and of the feelings of those around him. These exercises should also help parents and teachers see what it is like to be the object of demands or requests and, with their newly gained insights, act with more understanding.

At the start of each exercise, begin with the following induction: "Sit comfortably in a chair with your legs uncrossed. Your hands should be resting on your knees, palms up. Close your eyes and keep them closed until I tell you to open them. This helps us see things that we can't see with our eyes open. We will keep our eyes closed no more than two minutes. Now breathe out slowly through your mouth three times. Let me hear the sound of your breath coming out of your mouth as you slowly release the air."

> Note to Guide: Pause a couple of seconds to let the child finish breathing out, then begin with the exercise that you want the child to do. At the end of the exercise, pause very briefly and then say: "Breathe out once and open your eyes."

Exercise 82
See and hear an older brother or sister
Telling you what to do.

40

What is the reason they are telling this to you?

What do you do and how do you feel?

Exercise 83

Your friend phones, and you'd like to go and play,

But your mother says you have to watch your baby brother or
sister.

How do you work this out, and what do you feel?

Exercise 84

It seems to you that your little brother or sister

Can get away with everything,

But that you have to be on your best behavior at all times,

Because you are older and more is expected of you.

How do you feel?

What do you say or do?

Exercise 85

You sometimes feel resentful of your younger brother or sister.

Your parents tell you that because you are older

You also have more privileges.

Do you feel that this balances things out?

Can you explain to your parents how you feel?

What are you saying?

What are they telling you in return?

Exercise 86

Your older sister has a lot of makeup and jewelry.

One day when she is away, you try it on.

She comes home and is furious.

What is happening?

How does it all end?

Exercise 87

Your younger brother or sister tears up your homework.

This is not the first time

That you haven't brought your homework to school,

So the teacher doesn't believe you

And isn't interested in what you have to say.

What do you feel?

What do you do?

Exercise 88

You have to share a room with your younger brother or sister.

You wish you had your own room.

Tell the reason you want your own room.

What can you do?

Exercise 89

How does it feel to share your mother or father's love

With a newborn baby?

The baby seems to get the greater part of your parent's attention,

And this may make you feel unloved.

You feel they should be there for you alone —

But can they?

Exercise 90

See yourself being your big brother or sister.

Now see yourself being the baby in the family.

Now be yourself.

Who would you rather be?

What do you feel being this person?

Making Friends

"I have lots of friends, the whole class are my friends. Trouble is, nobody likes me."

—Jamal, age 11

Human beings are by nature social—people need people. In earliest infancy, you will notice that infants first play on their own, then side by side with other toddlers, and only later are they able to play together with one another. Failure to go through these important stages may detrimentally affect the ability to forge friendships later on in life. Children who don't have friends feel miserable, left out, and excluded. They become angry and sometimes resort to violence. Alternatively, they may turn their angry feelings inward and become self-destructive. The following exercises are geared towards helping children build friendships.

Exercise 91

See yourself wanting to be friends with somebody.

What do you do to be friends with this person?

Describe what happens.

Tell why you have picked this person to be your friend.

Exercise 92

See two children fighting.

Tell why they are fighting and what is happening.

Breathe out.

See yourself persuading one to stop the fighting.

How are you doing this?
Hear what you are saying.

Exercise 93
See yourself in a fight with one of your friends.
Perhaps he has called you a name.
Perhaps he has thought wrongly
That you have called him a name,
Although you haven't.
You feel extremely angry,
But part of you knows it is all a mistake
Due to a misunderstanding.
What are you doing?

Exercise 94
You hear one of the children in the class
Say something bad about your mother or father.
You get very angry and want to punch him,
But you know doing this will get you into trouble.
You decide not to get angry.
You breathe out slowly and quietly,
Walk away seeing how you have been king or queen of your
  actions.

Exercise 95
Close your eyes
And let any image or picture
Come into your mind.
Breathe out.
Let another image or picture come to you.

Exercise 96

See yourself sharing a favorite toy.

Tell what is happening.

With whom are you sharing your toy?

What are you feeling?

Exercise 97

See your friend sharing

A favorite toy with you.

What are you feeling?

Exercise 98

See yourself playing a game with a friend.

You win the game.

What are you feeling?

See yourself playing a game with a friend.

And this time you are losing.

What are you feeling?

Attracting Attention Negatively

Every child craves and needs attention. "Good" children may lose out on their fair share of attention merely because they're so good. Parents and teachers have to watch the trap of failing to give attention to good children, because ultimately the child may crave being noticed so much that he seeks it through negative ways. Conversely, children who are unable to live up to the expectations put upon them, both at home and in the classroom, act out in order to be noticed, no matter the price. In both of these cases, punishment is preferable to being ignored. If a child's needs continue to be ignored, he may turn into a bully.

Exercise 99

Imagine you want to get the teacher's attention.

You decide to call out in class.

You hear the teacher yelling at you.

You got her attention, but is this what you want?

See another way of getting her attention

Which will not hurt you.

Tell what is happening.

Exercise 100

Your mother is on the phone

With one of her friends.

You want her to help you with your homework.

You get into a fight with your sister,

And your mother sends you to your room.

You got her attention,

But is this what you want?

Imagine another way of getting your mother's attention

That will not hurt you.

Tell what is happening.

Exercise 101

You are mad because you feel ignored in class.

You push your classmate's books on the floor

And stomp on them.

The teacher sends you to the principal.

You get suspended for one day.

Now you're in trouble with your parents too.

Is this what you want?

What else could you have done to get attention?

Exercise 102

A classmate's books were thrown on the floor.

You decide to be nice and help pick them up.

The teacher compliments you in front of the whole class.

She appoints you her monitor for the week.

She also sends a letter home to your parents

Telling them how helpful you have been.

They buy you pizza and ice cream.

What are you learning from this?

The following exercises are geared towards helping children
put their life in order and attain inner equilibrium and balance.
Once this is acquired, parents will be better able to manage their
children, resulting in more harmony in the home.

Exercise 103

See yourself with a large canvas,

Painting a picture of a blue sky without clouds.

Put in large gold-yellow sunflowers drinking in the sun.

Put yourself in the picture.

See what is happening.

Exercise 104

Imagine you are polishing your shoes.

See everybody else in the class doing the same.

And see how the shoes look when polishing them and afterwards.

Bullying and Being Bullied

Dealing with the school bully is a problem that has plagued
parents, educators, teachers, social workers, and psychologists

for centuries. Bullying can be a minor nuisance or a problem of overwhelming proportion. The effects on the victim can be so disastrous as to make him school-phobic or even suicidal. The child who is the social outcast feels utterly miserable. In addition, the child who has a natural tendency towards timidity will have this trait reinforced. Consequently, he may suffer throughout his life by being unable to assert or defend himself. In the case of the bully, his actions stem from feelings of inadequacy and the need to gain power through putting others down. Instead of seeing this child as desperately in need of help, adults frequently punish the child, thereby reinforcing his feelings of inadequacy. Thus the cycle continues.

Here are some exercises to transform aggressive behavior on the part of the bully, and passivity on the part of the victim. The exercises help each child see himself and the other more objectively, thereby breaking the unconscious cycle between the aggressor and the victim.

Exercise 105
Imagine that you are a bully.
What are you doing?
To whom are you doing this?
Why have you chosen this particular person to bully?
Is there someone you would never bully?
Who is that person?
Why would you never bully him or her?

Exercise 106
Now see yourself being bullied.
Who is doing the bullying?

What are they doing?

Why are they doing it to you?

What are you feeling and what are you doing?

Kids making fun of me

Exercise 107

Hear another child calling you a name.

It could even be your brother or sister.

What name are they calling you?

How does this make you feel?

Hear yourself telling yourself the reason

The bully is calling you this name.

Is the reason because they want to annoy you?

Is the reason because they feel small and unimportant?

Knowing this, how do you respond?

Exercise 108

Be a cat chasing a mouse.

What is happening?

Be the mouse

And tell what is happening and how you feel.
Be the hole in the ground
Into which the mouse runs.
How does it feel to be this hole?

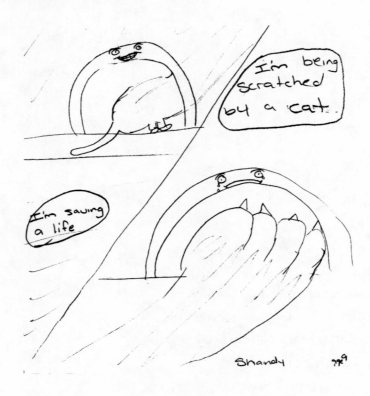

Exercise 109

Breathe out slowly three times.
Be a crocodile.
What or whom are you devouring?
What is happening?
How do you like it?

Exercise 110

Breathe out slowly three times.

Be a wolf stalking its prey.

You paw the earth,

And catch the little ground squirrel.

You hear the squeal

And walk away,

Prey in mouth.

What do you feel?

Child's Response

A person I don't like is Shakila. She is bossy. I don't know why I don't like her, so I close my eyes and pretend to be her to see how it feels to be bossy. When I try to be her, I found out why she was bossy. She is bossy because she is trying to make other people scared of her so that they can do things for her. If they would not be scared of her, they might ignore her, tell her to go away, or tell her to do it herself. She feels like nobody is her friend. I can see that people are bossy because they are afraid that no one will be their friend.

—Gary, age 10

The following exercises are for children who nag or disturb others, and who find pleasure in hurting others. It will also assist those who can't escape the nagger.

Exercise 111

You are a mosquito.

Tell how it is to be a mosquito.

Do you like it?

Exercise 112

You are an ant crawling on somebody's food.

What are you doing?

How are you feeling?

Tell what's happening.

Exercise 113

You are the bad one or the witch

In a fairy tale.

Tell how you feel

And what you do.

CHAPTER

3
Succeeding in School

"Experience is the father of wisdom;
memory is the mother."

—Anonymous

"I like imagery because it relaxes my brain and
lets my soul free. It's like I'm free from being
locked up for over 100 years."

— Carl

A problem I have is that if I study very
hard for a test and once I take it I fail
~~becase~~ because im nervous. Before the
test I no I really knew it, So when I
failed I was confused

I'm studying very hard.   I'm confused
My parents say study harder,

Sharpening Memory

Knowledge is built on knowledge. In order to go beyond, we have to remember what came before. So much of success in school and life is dependent on memory that it is a skill well worth acquiring. One sees programs for improving memory frequently in magazines and newspapers. These programs are geared to adults. But why wait until adulthood? With a few simple exercises done in a timely fashion, adults can do much to help children improve their memory function, which will enable children to be more successful in school. The goal is for each child to experience success in at least one subject area. This will do a great deal for the child's confidence and motivation. Following the induction are imagery exercises to help improve memory.

At the start of each exercise, begin with the following induction:

"Sit comfortably in a chair with your legs uncrossed. Your hands should be resting on your knees, palms up. Close your eyes and keep them closed until I tell you to open them. This helps us see things that we can't see with our eyes open. We will keep our eyes closed no more than two minutes. Now breathe out slowly through your mouth three times. Let me hear the sound of your breath coming out of your mouth as you slowly release the air."

> *Note to Guide: Pause a couple of seconds to let the child finish breathing out, then begin with the exercise that you want the child to do. At the end of the exercise, pause very briefly and then say: "Breathe out once and open your eyes."*

Exercise 114

See a tray with different objects on it.

See the tray being removed.

What are the objects you have seen?

Breathe out.

Why are those objects there?

Is there anything missing?

Is there anything there that is not necessary?

Exercise 115

Imagine it is Monday, and you are reading two lines of a poem.

It is a poem you like very much.

On Tuesday, you read four lines.

On Wednesday, five lines.

On Thursday, six lines.

On Friday, eight lines.

Imagine you have done this for three weeks.

See how your memory has improved.

Exercise 116

Imagine that you see on your TV screen all the moments when you
have had a bad reaction to someone in your family.

An example could be when you have been angry with your brother
or sister.

Breathe out.

Now see all the moments in the past that you have been angry with
your brother or sister.

Breathe out and imagine you are seeing all the moments you have
been nice to your brother or sister, beginning in childhood up to
this point.

Feel how you are enriching your memory with good feelings.

> *Note to Guide: By focusing on the good feelings when
> remembering the past, the memory is improved. At the same
> time, these exercises can help change the child's character,*

because they turn the focus towards the good and train the child to see what is good in himself and his surroundings.

Exercise 117

Imagine you are telling a story you have read
To your little brother or sister.
Breathe out.
Imagine that you take a story that you like very much
And make it into a play.
You act it out for the birthday of one of your friends,
Remembering all the roles, the sets, and the events.
Describe your play in detail.

Exercise 118

Make a game to find your shoe.
You have thrown it at your brother
And it fell out of a window.
You must hurry to school so as not to be late.
What happens when you arrive at school?

Exercise 119

When you go to bed, you can't find the pants of your pajamas.
You cannot go to bed without them.
What do you do?
How do you feel?

> *Note to Guide: The child must go backward in her mind to find the shoe or pajamas. Going backward helps improve the memory.*

Exercise 120

See yourself eating breakfast.

Tell what you have eaten.

Look again and see if there is something you left out.

Tell the ingredients of every part of your breakfast.

Exercise 121

See what you ate for supper last night.

Tell what you ate and what you left on your plate.

Make sure not to leave anything out.

Now, picture what you will eat tonight for supper,

And see if you can taste what is on your plate.

Exercise 122

See again your first day at school.

See what you were wearing.

How was the teacher dressed?

How did the teacher seem to you?

How did the room look?

Tell how you felt.

> *Note to Guide: Exercise 122 is difficult. If the child can do it, he will make fast progress.*

Exercise 123

Remember the first story your mother or teacher told you.

Hear yourself telling it to a friend.

How did the story begin?

How did it end?

Improving School Grades

So much time of a child's life is spent in school. If a child does well in school, all is well, but what about the child who is a poor student? Symptoms appear all too quickly—boredom, disruptiveness, lack of motivation, psychosomatic syndromes, school phobia, or poor school attendance. Some children fall asleep in class because they don't hear or see well or because they think the teacher doesn't like them. This may also be true of underachievers even if the cause of their failure is not known.

If left untreated too long, these problems may be almost impossible to correct. Exercises to help improve memory, decrease impulsiveness, and let a child experience success at something— no matter what—are all effective in helping children succeed at school. Children who learn to maximize their abilities early on will be able to apply what they have learned to the rest of their lives. Practicing the following exercises can be of great assistance.

Exercise 124

Close your eyes and breathe out slowly three times.
Remember a time you felt really proud of yourself.
Imagine this same situation is happening to you now.
Tell what is happening.

Exercise 125

You are in your classroom.
See and hear your teacher praising you for something you did.
It may be for answering a question correctly.
It may be for sitting nicely in your seat.
It may be for helping another child.
Tell how it feels to be praised by the teacher.

What did you do to deserve to be praised?

See yourself going home and telling your mother what the teacher
   said.

How does it feel?

Ms. Berkovits told me A Trik. how To see the words on A screen in my mind. I opened my eyes And tried to see A screeen And said iT And spelled it. I got A 48. Next week I got A 100 I feel Proud I got A 0 befor The Trik.

Lyndell
Age 9

Exercise 126

See yourself getting a good grade in a subject.

What subject is it?

For what reasons do you get good grades in this subject?

Could you make these reasons apply to other subjects?

How?

Exercise 127

Breathe out.

See yourself getting a poor grade in a subject.

What subject is it?

See and hear yourself telling yourself

The reason you are getting a poor grade.

Breathe out.

Now hear yourself telling yourself

What you need to do to get a good grade.

What are you saying?

What do you do?

Exercise 128

Picture yourself doing the things you have heard

You need to do to get a good grade.

See yourself getting the good grade you want.

Now picture yourself doing this again, and again, and again.

And know that the teacher gives you the grade

That you determine to get.

Exercise 129

Decide what grade you want

For a particular test or piece of homework.

See yourself knowing the answers

And writing with assurance and confidence.

Breathe out.

Now see yourself receiving the work back from the teacher.

See clearly the grade you want written on your paper.

Understand how believing in yourself

Brings out the best in you.

Exercise 130

Which would you rather have:

A strict but fair teacher?

A caring but shouting teacher?

A young or old teacher?

An old, pretty teacher

Or a young, unattractive one?

Tell the reasons for your choice.

> *Note to Guide: The following exercise can be used to help children with memory retention in practically any subject, from remembering spelling words in reading class, to multiplication tables in math class.*

Jeff
4-203   Grade 4

Once thir was a lady name mrs. Bercovits.
she taught us about time tables. We learn a fun
way. on our brain. after we saw it. we put it in
our brain. an we amagined it on a screen
in our brain. then we feed it from the screen.
with our eyes closed. it was fun quick and
easy.
      Age 10

now I now my
seven times tables
I am a winner?

61

Exercise 131
Imagine you have a screen inside your head.
See yourself writing your spelling words on the screen.
Now read the words that you have written on your screen.
Read them forwards and then read them backwards.
Now that you have put the words inside your head,
You can read them when you take a test,
And get them all right.

Children's Responses
A teacher who is strict but fair I would prefer over one who is
lenient but fair because if she is strict that would mean that she
really cares about her class because a strict teacher will pull up
on you and it will be for your own good and you will be more
disciplined in life. You will learn more, you might not have as
much fun but at least you are learning.

—Melissa, age 12

My teacher said, "Let's learn the six times tables." I close my
eyes and I wrote it on my screen in my head. And then I saw the
answers. But you can't see them unless you want to see it. And if
you don't want to see it, it just doesn't pop up. Like times tables or
anything else.

Now I know if you really want to learn, you got to do it this way,
'cause the other ways takes long. This way is the easiest. This way
you got to concentrate on doing it, and if you really concentrate,
you could do it fast and easy.

—Nelson, age 9

Ms. Berkooits told me a trick—how to see the words on a screen in my mind. As I opened my eyes and tried to see a screen and said the word and spelled it, I got a 48. Next week, I got 100. I feel proud. I got a zero before the trick.

—Lyndell, age 9

Developing Patience and Stick-to-It-iveness

If children are to succeed to the best of their ability, they must acquire perseverance and patience. Many children are impatient and give up trying early on, because they don't see immediate results or because the results they do see seem to be insignificant. This can be a major cause of failure. Even some bright children fail because they are impatient. The following exercises can help children learn to cultivate patience and perseverance in whatever they do, allowing them to succeed in school and in life.

Exercise 132

You plant a seed.

You water it daily.

It appears that nothing is happening.

But you know differently.

You continue to take care of it,

Trusting and believing.

Then one day you see a tiny green shoot.

You patiently water the little shoot

Until first one leaf,

Then another, grows.

You continue to water and care for the little plant.

One day you see a little bud

Waiting to open.

It is not yet time.

You know you cannot force it.
It will be a flower
In its own good time.

Exercise 133
You are eating your favorite meal very slowly.
How does it feel in your mouth?
How does it taste?

Exercise 134
You are watching the water run into the bathtub.
Very slowly, it trickles in.
What feelings are you having?

Exercise 135
You are a red traffic light that doesn't seem to change—
What thoughts and feelings are going on in your mind?

Exercise 136
You have done your homework.
Your baby brother or sister has ripped it into many pieces.
You patiently gather all the pieces up,
Put them in place, and one by one stick them together.
What are your feelings?

Exercise 137
You get a birthday present a week before your birthday,
But you may not open it now.
How do you manage to wait until you can open it?

Exercise 138

Your favorite aunt comes to visit from abroad.

You are impatient to see what she has brought for you.

But she is too tired to unpack her suitcase.

What are you doing?

Prioritizing and Putting Things in Place

Sensing when something is out of place then recognizing what adjustments are needed and making them is a valuable skill for children in both life and school. In order to succeed—particularly in school—one must have a good sense of order about what should come first, second, third, and so on. Order in the physical realm often helps one achieve mental and emotional order.

Exercise 139

Have your shoes on the wrong foot.

You walk around like this.

Tell how it feels.

Exercise 140

You are wearing one high-heeled shoe and one flat shoe.

What is the effect on your body and on your mood?

Does it have an effect on your work?

Exercise 141

You are wearing a sweater or a dress with the back in the front.

Go about your day like this.

What is happening, and how does it feel?

Breathe out slowly.

You are wearing your sweater or dress inside out.

How does it feel different between inside out and back to front?

Exercise 142

You are wearing clothes whose colors do not match.

How are you feeling?

What is happening?

What do you do?

Exercise 143

See yourself eating breakfast at night.

How does it feel? Breathe out slowly.

See yourself eating dinner in the morning.

What does this do to your day?

Exercise 144

Imagine your week starting out with any day you like.

Give your reasons for choosing this day.

Child's Response

Dinner for breakfast would be yuck if we had mashed potatoes and steak. Breakfast for dinner would be great if we had eggs and toast. I think it would be great if we had breakfast for dinner. I would hate it if we had dinner for breakfast. So breakfast in the morning and breakfast in the evening, that would be great!

—Odessa, age 10

Curbing and Controlling Impulsiveness

Spontaneity is a quality we often find in children. However, in its negative form, it manifests itself as impulsivity. Impulsivity, if left untamed, may get the child into trouble: either endangering himself or another or hampering his learning in some way. The following exercises are geared towards helping the child slow down, develop patience, and gain inner peace. The child who learns to do this maintains his strength, energy, and power, which can then be harnessed and directed. In cases where children fail to do this, they dissipate their strength and do not obtain the desired results from their efforts. These exercises are intended to help children restrain their impulsivity, enabling them to succeed.

Exercise 145

Watch a piece of ice melting slowly.
See how it becomes smaller and smaller.
See how its shape is changing.
Notice the puddle of water becomes bigger
As the ice becomes smaller.
What are you sensing and feeling?

Exercise 146

Hold a pendulum in your hands.
Watch it move back and forth
Until it slowly comes to a standstill.
Pay attention to what is happening inside your body.

Exercise 147

Sit and listen to your breathing,
In and out, in and out.
Pay attention to your rhythm and balance.
Sense it in your body.
Tell what effect it has.

Exercise 148

You have a box of watercolors in front of you.

The colors are all very bright, but you want pastels.

Take bright red and water it down

Until it is the right shade of light pink you want.

Now do this with the other colors.

Sense what is happening in your body.

Exercise 149

See yourself holding in your hand

A glass containing a drink you like very much.

You are very thirsty, but instead of gulping it down,

You sip it slowly.

Notice what is happening.

Exercise 150

There's a stain on your skirt or pants and you're washing it out.

You keep rubbing and rubbing, but it is stubborn

And only gets a little lighter.

What are you doing and feeling?

Do you succeed in the end in removing it?

Exercise 151

See yourself entering a room,

Wanting to open a drawer,

But refraining from opening it.

What are you feeling?

You want to touch everything that is on the table,

But you stop yourself from doing it.

What are you feeling now?

Exercise 152

Imagine you are entering a room

You have never been in before.

See yourself looking at everything in the room,

Wanting to touch but not touching.

Tell what you are seeing and not touching.

Tell what is on the table.

Open one drawer and tell what is inside.

If you take anything out,

Return it to its place

And tell again what is inside the drawer.

Eliminating Distractions

People have a natural tendency to distract themselves from what's important in their lives. These exercises are intended to help children figure out what is really good for them, whether or not they want it, and how to focus on and achieve their desired outcome.

Exercise 153

Have a bag.

Throw into it all the things that distract you.

Be aware of what these things are.

Put the bag behind you.

Exercise 154

Breathe out.

Each time you breathe out,

Breathe out one thing that distracts you,

That you are thinking about,

Instead of doing your work.

As you breathe out

Know that you are letting the distraction go,

And see yourself completing your work.

Exercise 155

See the air that you breathe out

Become a balloon.

What color is your balloon?

Put a distraction in your balloon.

See the wind carry your balloon high up and away.

Now see yourself doing your work without distractions.

Tell what distraction you put in your balloon.

Exercise 156

Imagine you are polishing an old silver cup.

Keep polishing and polishing

Until you are able to see your own reflection.

Look closely and read the message that is there for you.

Now look inside the cup and tell what is inside.

Exercise 157

You're watching a piece of soap melting in water.

You play with it and make bubbles.

As you watch it slowly disappearing,

Notice your sensations.

Exercise 158

See a volcano erupting.

Tell what it looks like, what it feels like, and what it sounds like.

Now have a magic jug of water
And pour it over the head of the volcano to quiet it.
Sense how you are quieting it.
Sense how you are quieting yourself by quieting the volcano.

Exercise 159
Sense and feel how it is to be lightning and thunder.
Hear the loud crash of the thunder.
See the bright flash of the lightning.
How does it feel to be lightning and thunder?

Exercise 160
Be the sun coming out after the rain.
Be the rain coming out after the sun.
Which do you like being better?
Give your reasons why.

I See This Wen I amm mad

"I DON'T KNOW WHAT IT IS." Nelson

4

Getting in Touch with Your Inner Guide

*"You know I'm the tallest in the class, and I'm
smart, but I'm still scared to walk down the
stairs by myself."*

—Johnny, age 5

Conquering Fear

Fear is one of the crucial characteristics for survival. It can trigger
the "fight or flight" response in a dangerous situation. However,
when fear becomes misplaced or exaggerated, it can inhibit a
child's development. In order to conquer fear, the child must first
enter into the fear. Once the child becomes acquainted with his
fear, then he can find the light that will help him overcome it.

Exercise: Overcoming Fear

Sheila, grade 8, age 13, is an A+ student in every way, but
something told me that she could use counseling. I felt that perhaps
she was too good, too dutiful, too compliant. When I asked her
teacher if I could see her I met with a lot of resistance. "She's a
perfect student," I was told, "and there's no reason why you should
want to see her." "Perhaps she's too much of a perfect student," I
said. "Too much of anything is not good." Reluctantly her teacher
allowed her to come for one session.

Sheila told me that she had some fears that she wanted to talk
about. I asked her to close her eyes and look inside her body to see
where her fear was residing.

Counselor: See where in your body your fear is.

Sheila: I see fear as black. I also see it as sarcasm.

Counselor: Could you tell me what you mean by that?

Sheila: Bad things people say about you.

Counselor: Like what?

Sheila: She's so weird, she acts funny, she's strange — how she walks, how she talks. I also see it as a kind of death.

Counselor: Can you tell me a little bit more about that?

Sheila: You're young, and you fear you might die at age twelve or thirteen or fourteen.

Counselor: Why do you have fears like this?

Sheila: I worry too much.

Counselor: Do you know someone who died at that age?

Sheila: No.

Counselor: Do you fear you might die?

Sheila: Yeah. I might die.

Counselor: What makes you think you might die?

Sheila: The wrong things I do.

Counselor: Like what?

Sheila: Like overhearing conversations between my mom and a friend of hers, when I think they are talking about me. And butting into conversations.

Counselor: What else do you do that you think is bad?

Sheila: Not remembering to say thank you and forgetting to brush my teeth.

Counselor: Anything else?

Sheila: That's all.

Counselor: It seems to me that you are like the rest of us. We try to do what's right, but inevitably we all slip up from time to time. That includes me; that includes your teachers; and that includes your parents. We generally don't slip up on purpose, but we do slip up. It's the way human beings are, imperfect. Perfection is only to be found in angels and God.

Sheila: So I'm not a very bad person?

Counselor: You are a very normal person. You try to do what's good, and most of the time you succeed. Sometimes you make an error or a little mistake. Sometimes you forget something. Generally, you don't do this on purpose. It happens. It happens to you; it happens to me; it happens to most people.

Sheila: So I'm like everybody else?

Counselor: Yes, you're like everybody else. Human. There's one more thing I want to tell you. It's important to distinguish between small errors and big errors, between doing something on purpose and doing it by mistake. They are not at all the same thing. Forgetting to say thank you or occasionally forgetting to brush your teeth is not the same as deliberately hurting someone's feelings or deliberately stealing. Do you see the difference?

Sheila: Yes. Hurting someone's feelings or stealing are much worse.

Counselor: That's right. And even if you did those things you still wouldn't deserve to die. You'd need to look at what you did and repair it, by returning the thing you stole and apologizing to the person whose feelings you hurt. Then you'd have to resolve not to do these things again. And it would be over.

Sheila: I get it, you can undo the wrong thing and then do the right thing.

Counselor: That's right. I see you understand perfectly. Now I want you to do one more thing before going back to class. I'd like you to close your eyes and imagine that a friend of yours has the fears that you talked to me about today, and you are counseling her. What would you say to your friend?

Sheila: I'd say, "You have too much fear in you. All you have to do is ask God and pray to God. Whatever bad situation you're in, He will help you, and He will guide you to a new you that is fear-free. You'll have confidence in yourself and people will love you better."

Counselor: How do you feel now?

Sheila: Great.

Counselor: Try to be more precise.

Sheila: Nurtured.

In conducting an exercise I try not to accept overworked words, for example, nice, great, wonderful, etc. Generally, by prodding just a little, the kids do come up with words and expressions that are more precise. When I ask them to be specific, I notice great improvement in their writing, artwork, acuity, and depth of perception. In general, they express themselves far more creatively than before their imagery experience.

At the start of each exercise, begin with the following induction:

"Sit comfortably in a chair with your legs uncrossed. Your hands should be resting on your knees, palms up. Close your eyes and keep them closed until I tell you to open them. This helps us see things that we can't see with our eyes open. We will keep our eyes closed no more than two minutes. Now breathe out slowly through your mouth three times. Let me hear the sound of your breath coming out of your mouth as you slowly release the air."

> *Note to Guide: Pause a couple of seconds to let the child finish breathing out, then begin with the exercise that you want the child to do. At the end of the exercise, pause very briefly and then say: "Breathe out once and open your eyes."*

These exercises can help a child overcome fear where it is inappropriate, and enable him to relax and feel secure.

Exercise 161
See and sense a stone inside your chest.
Reach out your hands to the sun
And let the sun warm your hands and make them full of light.
With your hands full of light from the sun
You gradually enlarge your throat and your chest.
You put your hands of light inside you
And take out the stone and throw it behind you.
Now very gently you massage the area
Where the stone was,
Bringing light and healing to this place.

> *Note to Guide: The following exercise expands on the previous one.*

Exercise 162

See yourself standing in front of two mirrors.

In one mirror you see your spine very straight, clear, and healthy.

In the other mirror you see the stone in the middle of your chest.

Now with your hands full of light,

Slowly enlarge your throat and chest.

Remove the stone and throw it behind you.

Massage delicately the place where the stone was

To remove any trace or shadow that has been left by the stone.

Sense the space inside you and accept the light.

Exercise 163

You find yourself doing one thing you were frightened of in the
  past.

You tell yourself that now you are stronger, braver, wiser.

What is the thing you were frightened of?

How do you feel when doing it now?

Exercise 164

You see a black spider crawling and you are not scared.

You decide not to be scared.

You look at it closely to see the beauty of the web.

What are you learning from this?

Entering into the Fear

The exercises in this section help children enter into their worst
fears, anxieties, or worries. Through entering these dark parts,
they discover the hopes and dreams that are hidden within the
fear as well as magical qualities of brightness and optimism. Even
in the darkest moments one should not feel frightened. There is

always some light one can bring into the dark. These exercises help children bring a little light into dark places.

Exercise 165

You are closed in a box.

What are you doing?

Describe the box.

Describe yourself.

Describe your feelings.

Describe how you get out.

Exercise 166

You lock yourself into a dark closet.

How does it feel?

Breathe out.

Someone locks you in a dark closet.

Tell how this is different from when you lock yourself in.

Exercise 167

Imagine yourself in a dark cupboard.

Are you alone?

How did you get there?

Did you put yourself inside it?

What are you thinking and what are you feeling?

Breathe out.

Bring a little light in this cupboard.

What do you see?

How do you feel now that there is a little light?

Breathe out.

Now bring even more light inside the cupboard.

It is still dark, but there is a fair amount of light.

More things become apparent.

What do you see that you didn't see before?

Tell what is happening and what you feel.

Breathe out.

Do you wish to stay in the cupboard any longer?

Or do you wish to come out?

How do you find your way out?

Tell what you see when you come out.

Finding Light through the Fear

Children can be blinded by overwhelming fear, which may
paralyze their ability to find their own particular light. Having
conquered fear in the previous exercises, children are now able to
re-enter "the box." This time they can enter fearlessly because they
now have the ability to bring light in.

Exercise 168

You are in a little box.

How does it feel to be in this little box?

Tell what is happening.

If you feel fearful, bring a little light into this little box.

With a little light, a little lamp, or a flashlight in your hand,

You can see how to get out.

Tell how you get out of the box.

Exercise 169

You are hiding from your friends or the teacher in a dark closet.

Tell what is happening.

What are you feeling?

What are you thinking?

What are you doing?

Tell how it all ends.

Children's Responses

Boyce, age 11, a fifth-grade student from the special ed unit of a large urban public school, responded to The Box exercise with, "It feels fun being in the box. It's like you make a clubhouse and you get in and it's hard to get out. We was pushing and pushing, and then we couldn't get out. We shouted, 'Help, help!' Then some guys came and we were still stuck, they couldn't get us out. It was like you was in a jail. And then I kicked the wall with both of my feet and the wood fell down and everybody ran out saying, 'We're free, we're free, no more jail.' We was running around, playing games and everything. And then we made another clubhouse. We didn't get locked in. We made it all better. We made a lock with a hole and a key."

Lyndell, from the same class, experienced The Box exercise as, "It's not a box; it's a cage. It feels locked up. There's no light but it doesn't feel dark. I didn't get out at all. Someone was aiming a gun at me. It makes me feel like dead. I stay there for a million years." Omar, almost eleven years old, gave the following script to The Box exercise:

I'm in a box.

The box is brown.

I'm trying to get out.

I'm going, "Help me, help me!"

I'm crying, "Get me out!"

It's too dark in there. I can't see.

The guards put iron on me.

They put iron on the box.
I'm saying, "Help me, help me!"
I'm dying of thirst,
I'm hungry,
I'm struggling.
And one time I just got tired. And I was hungry and I couldn't
  hardly breathe.
I was almost dying.
So I had to just get out of there.
The guards were sleeping.
I just burst the box open.

As you can tell by reading the above three responses, some
children are able to find more light and break free from the
box, while others feel trapped and imprisoned—by themselves,
by others, or by a combination of both. Boyce learns from his
mistakes and improves his situation the next time around. Lyndell's
response to the exercise is one of extreme passivity. He feels
powerless. Although he isn't dead, he "feels like dead" and takes
no action to get out of the box. This exercise reflects his life, as he
is extremely complacent and shows no interest or involvement in
schoolwork. In Omar's case, he keeps trying to get out by using
his voice. Although he fails repeatedly, he doesn't think of trying
other methods. He also makes the situation worse by installing
guards. However, when he becomes very desperate, he finds a way
to succeed.

The Negative Emotions of Frustration and Anger

If frustration is left to fester, it can lead to resentment, which in
turn can lead to an embittered, sour personality. Resentment is part
of the cycle of anger, guilt, and fear, which needs to be cleansed

from the personality. Some of these emotions, such as anger, provide the body with extra energy but are not helpful for everyday life. Fear and anger are defenses for survival—they balance all other tendencies. Anger is something active; fear is not. When one wants to fight, the fueling emotion is anger. When one wants to flee, the fueling emotion is fear. The following exercises help children understand and accept that in life they cannot always have their own way.

Exercise 170
See yourself in the classroom.
The boy or girl next to you, or in front of you, or behind you,
Is not paying attention to the teacher.
What is going on?
Hear this child saying, "I don't care."
What do you think that child is really feeling?
Why might he be saying, "I don't care?"

Exercise 171
Imagine you are this child who is not paying attention.
Hear yourself saying, "I don't care."
Why are you saying this?
What would you like the teacher to say or do?
Breathe out.
You are the best friend of this child.
What are you saying or doing to help him?

Exercise 172
Picture yourself doing a puzzle.
One piece doesn't fit.
You try this and you try that.
Still it doesn't fit.

What are you doing?

What are you feeling?

Exercise 173

You want to play with a certain toy,

But your younger brother or sister wants it.

Your mother says, "He is a baby, give it to him."

How do you feel?

What do you do?

Exercise 174

You have given the toy to your baby brother or sister.

You see they have broken it.

How do you feel and what do you do?

Exercise 175

You are a bird building a nest.

Tell where you are building your nest.

What materials are you using?

Describe your nest when it is finished.

Breathe out.

You fly away,

And when you return, another bird is in your nest.

What do you feel?

What is happening?

Exercise 176

Just as you finish building your nest,

A storm comes and destroys it.

What do you feel?

What do you do?

Child's Response

If I were the bird I would feel very angry but I would start over because, after all, they are my baby birds, and I would want to protect them. I learned that I am willing to work hard to protect something important to me.

— Max, age 11

The following exercises help children better deal with the emotion of anger.

This is my anger its big and sharp. I'm going to take it and get some gum and stick it on my anger then take it and put it on the sidewalk. Now I feel fantastic cause I get rid of my anger. Now I feel great cause I don't have to deal with it any more.

Exercise 177

Think of someone who makes or made you angry.

Instead of getting into a fight,

See yourself blowing out your anger.

See it as a cloud.

Tell what color it is.

Breathe out.

See the cloud being carried by the wind up into the sky

And turning into a star.

What is happening to your feelings?

Tell me where you are.

If you're up, come down in a ray of light.

Know that this is your star and it is always shining for you!

See if you can hear the melody of your star.

What do you feel?

10 Years

Jennifer

When I feel anar I kick my Things around the place, I jump on my bed, I Slam the door in my Brothers Face, I cars out the window. and I screm.

What will I Do whidth my angar I roll it up into one big Ball and I thow it to kanose city.

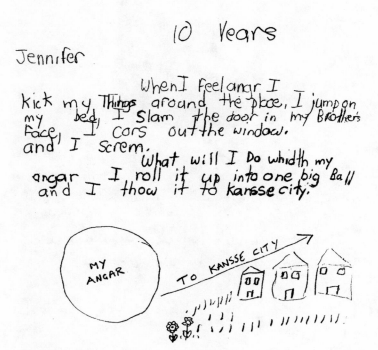

Exercise 178

See and hear a child doing or saying something to annoy you.

What is he doing?

What is he saying?

Why do you think he is saying or doing this?

How are you reacting?

Breathe out.

Are you losing your temper?

Is there something else you would rather do?

Tell what it is that you would rather do.

Letting Go of Guilt

The guilt that we feel as adults may have begun in childhood. Therefore it is good to clear it out in childhood. If not, it may stay undetected and become the cause of much suffering and pain, remaining with us for many years. The longer the guilt stays, the more damaging it can become, sometimes causing physical and emotional illness. It is important to adopt a healthy attitude towards guilt, to express remorse for wrongdoing, and move on with life. Staying frozen in guilt does no one any good.

The punitive approach that adults sometimes take towards childhood misdemeanors, such as lying and stealing, often increases the unwanted behavior. If the child feels unloved, feelings of unworthiness and guilt may prompt him to lie or steal even more. Setting standards based on understanding rather than punishment are more likely to result in the desired behavior because the adult accepts the child and does not alienate him.

Stealing is usually a sign that the child feels a lack of affection. The adult has to make it clear that he loves the child but not what the child has done. The child has done wrong and needs to know that.

Sometimes children lie because they feel small and inadequate. They want to impress others with their importance. Children want to look big. They think it helps them gain popularity when they boast of their wonderful parents, their riches and possessions, and so they exaggerate their wealth. Children may describe their father's car, turning it from an old Ford into a Lincoln, a Mercedes, or a BMW. With time and proper education, they can learn that the best thing is to be content with being true to themselves.

The following exercises are designed to increase the child's understanding of himself and the adult's understanding of the child in situations in which the child has not acted appropriately. The exercises also help the child clear out his guilty feelings and enable him to move on with life.

Exercise 179
See yourself reading a list of things you did in the past
That you wish you hadn't done or feel you should not have done.
Hear yourself telling yourself that you were little
When this happened and didn't know better.
Know that everybody makes mistakes
And the main thing is to repair them
And not repeat them.

Exercise 180
See yourself in a park.
See the beautiful lawns and flowerbeds.
There are signs saying:
"Do not walk on the grass."
"Do not pick the flowers."
But you do walk on the grass and you do pick the flowers.

You think nobody is looking.
What do you feel?

Exercise 181
See yourself in a grocery store.
You want ice cream, but you have no money.
You manage to distract the owner and take an ice cream.
You hide it under your coat as you walk out of the store.
How do you feel?

Exercise 182
You are angry at your mother for not having more time for you
Because there's a new baby in the family,
Or a younger brother or sister needs her attention.
In your heart you curse your mother.
Know that you did it out of anger.
Know that when we are angry we do things we don't really mean.
Know that you didn't mean it.

Exercise 183
Remember a time you cheated on a test,
Copied somebody else's homework,
Or told a lie.
Remember how frightened you felt that you would fail or get into
  trouble
And that's why you did what you did.
When we're frightened we sometimes do things we don't
  normally do.
When we lack the courage to be honest, we may act dishonestly.
Know that sometimes being honest takes courage.

Exercise 184

See yourself getting caught for something

You know you shouldn't have done,

And thought you wouldn't get caught for.

You feel the need to save face and hear yourself saying:

"I didn't do it, he did."

"She started."

"It fell down by itself."

"I didn't lose it, someone took it away from me."

Recognize that deep down you feel guilty

And you are saying this in order to stay out of trouble.

Understand that if we all continually told lies,

We would never know what is real.

We would never know whom to trust or what to believe.

Forgiving Others and Yourself

"To err is human, to forgive divine."

—Alexander Pope

Forgiving is difficult for children; although they might forget
sooner than adults, their strict sense of justice may not allow them
to forgive easily. If they do learn to forgive, they will be free
from their guilt, and their relationships throughout their lives will
benefit. The following exercises will help children learn how to
forgive.

Exercise 185

Think of someone who upset or hurt you.

It could be your mother or father,

Or brother or sister or teacher or friend.

See and hear them telling you they are sorry.

They did not mean to hurt you.

But sometimes they don't know what to do,

Themselves, when they make an error

Or respond harshly to you.

Hear them telling you they love you.

Hear them asking you to forgive them.

Do you forgive them?

If so, tell how.

Exercise 186

Think of someone you have hurt.

See him or her in front of you.

Hear yourself telling them

You sometimes do things you regret afterwards.

You are sometimes careless or thoughtless

Or impulsive or impatient

Or you lose your temper.

Tell them you are sorry and ask them to forgive you.

Exercise 187

Think of someone you love who has hurt you.

See them in front of you.

See the act they did that hurt.

Relive that moment of hurt again.

Feel how that hurt felt.

Breathe out.

Know they didn't do it to be evil or mean,

But acted out of their limitations.

Recognize what this limitation is.

Knowing this, does it make any difference
In how you feel about them?
See how it makes a difference
In how you feel about yourself.

Exercise 188
See and hear yourself saying:
"I forgive myself for things I took I should not have taken."
"I forgive myself for things I did I should not have done."
"I forgive myself for things I said I should not have said."
"I forgive myself for things I did not say I should have said."
"I forgive myself for things I did not do that I should have done."

Sharpening and Shaping Intuition

We all have a natural sense of intuition and we may be very
much in touch with it, particularly when we are children. As we
age, however, we can lose touch with our intuition through the
everyday influences of our society and its values. These exercises
can help children acquire and sharpen their intuition and become
more aware of it so they will not lose it as they age.

Exercise 189
See yourself sitting on top of a tree.
Look around from this new and different perspective.
You know what you need now to do and where you have to go.

Exercise 190
Imagine you are riding on the wings of a very wise bird.
The bird is whispering to you, telling you
What to do to help yourself.

Thank the bird

And see yourself beginning to do these things.

Exercise 191

You enter into a cave full of light.

There is a wise man inside this cave

Waiting to tell you what you need to do next.

What does he say?

Exercise 192

Inside the cave there is now a fake wise man,

Who tells you what may seem good but really isn't.

Hear what he says and tell why it is not good.

Tell this one to go away—and not to come back.

Exercise 193

You are inside your foot and see yourself walking.

Now you are in your big toe.

You walk around in it, and it begins to grow and grow and grow,

Making a path straight ahead of you.

When you have found where it leads to, return back.

Developing the Inner Conscience

Both adults and children have an inner conscience—the still, clear voice that we have inside ourselves and that we hear only when we make the effort to block out the distractions we tend to focus on. Generally, if we do succeed in hearing and listening to the inner voice, it has good, sound advice for us. The trick is to know that we have this inner conscience. The next step is to access it.

Teachers and parents can help children become aware of their inner conscience and can train them to observe themselves and modify their behavior. This inner conscience can also help children deal with conflicts within themselves and manage their feelings and desires. It also helps them deal with external conflicts, such as conflicts between what the child wants to do and what others want of the child and conflicts between wanting to do the right thing but also wanting to please others. Here are some exercises to help children pay attention to their inner conscience: the part of us which really knows and that we have to learn to trust—the wisdom of the heart.

Exercise 194

Be still and listen to your breathing.

Pay attention to the natural rhythm of your breathing.

Sense the inner calm that you feel.

Hear the inside voice,

And know that this is your inner conscience.

Exercise 195

Sense your inner conscience.

Know that your inner conscience is your best friend,

Who wants only what is best for you.

Ask it what you should do in order to succeed better

In one day, in one week, in one month.

Exercise 196

Ask your inner conscience

What you have now to do, be, or imagine

To be able to succeed in three days, and in one week.

Exercise 197

Hear your inner conscience telling you

How you can succeed now

To get along better

With your parents or brother or sister

Or with your teachers.

Breathe out.

In your schoolwork.

Breathe out.

With yourself.

What is it telling you?

Do you know the reason it is telling you this?

Exercise 198

What are some things your inner conscience is telling you to do?

And what are the things it is telling you not to do?

Exercise 199

Remember to talk to your inner conscience every day.

Hear what it has to say.

If you need advice about something specific, ask it.

It has good suggestions for you

And will never let you down.

Remember to thank it for its help

And for caring about you.

Exercise 200

Know that your inner conscience

Is always there and aware of what is happening to you.

It will answer you if you ask with respect

And trust that the answer will come.

Exercise 201

Know that your inner conscience

Knows you better than anyone else

And knows what is really the best for you.

Exercise 202

You may want to give your inner conscience-friend a name.

What is the name you have chosen?

CHAPTER

5
Exploring Your Unique Self

"Guided imagery lets me be whatever I want to be. I could see me as a birthday present. I could see myself as a baby doll and the girls are playing with me."

—Cindy, age 9

Colors

These exercises will help children see how different colors make them feel, and will show them how they can use color to change how they feel or change their mood of the day. Wearing different colors may change the child's perception of herself, as well as how others perceive her, and this can then change the child's interactions with the people around her. In a pilot experiment, researchers found that people who wore red tended to be more outgoing, while those who wore blue were less assertive. In this chapter, children can learn what effect colors have on them. The exercises give them an opportunity to experiment with the colors they wear, trying new combinations to see their effects.

Here are some exercises to help children become more aware of color in their world, enabling them to surround themselves with the colors they like, so they feel good.

At the start of each exercise, begin with the following induction:

"Sit comfortably in a chair with your legs uncrossed. Your hands should be resting on your knees, palms up. Close your eyes and keep them closed until I tell you to open them. This helps us see things that we can't see with our eyes open. We will keep our eyes closed no more than two minutes. Now breathe out slowly through your mouth three times. Let me hear the sound of your breath coming out of your mouth as you slowly release the air."

Note to Guide: Pause a couple of seconds to let the child finish breathing out, and then begin with the exercise that you want the child to do. At the end of the exercise, pause very briefly and then say: "Breathe out once and open your eyes."

Exercise 203
Be any color you want to be.
What color are you choosing?
What are you feeling by being this color?
What can you do by being this color
That you couldn't do before?

Exercise 204
Be a color you don't like.
What color are you choosing?
What are you feeling and sensing when you are this color?

Exercise 205
Imagine you're wearing your favorite color for a day.
How are you feeling wearing this color?
What are you able to do?
Tell how your day goes.
What difference does your favorite color make in your day?

Terrance   5- 116
        Blue and I
I clows my eyes and I
bereath out slowly and I
emagn the coler Blue, dark blue
and I like That coler very mdch
I wore That coler all the Time.
My coler remines me of Ice,
and of the ochen.
Snow is Icey blue, and the skiye
is blue to. It peles good and
exsteing to be blue.

Children's Responses

I was wearing my favorite color purple, a light purple. Before I
didn't feel free but on this day I do. I can express myself more. I
couldn't do that before. People look at me a little bit different, as if
I had become a better person. The day is a cool spring day. Flowers
are blooming, and the world doesn't feel dangerous anymore. It
feels so wonderful. The rest of the day was perfect too. My two
favorite groups, Kriss Kross and Jodeci, came to see the people on
my block. Then the day ended. I had to take off my color purple. I
felt sad that I had to take off my favorite colored clothes.

—Deanna, age 10

My favorite color is red. When I wear red, I feel good, I feel like
a millionaire. I also feel like a superstar. When I wear red, I feel I

can go anywhere I want. I feel like I am the most expensive person in America. When I wear red, I breathe in the beautiful scent of the flowers. I love to wear red because of its rich feelings.

—Charlene, age 11

When I wear my favorite color violet, I feel free and relaxed and respected. People compliment me and say that I look pretty and charming.

—Cassandra, age 10

Shapes

Shape influences how we see our physical selves in relationship to the world. Many children respond very well and vividly to the shape exercises. Some of their actual responses were as follows: "I felt squeezed as a cube." "I felt like I was an eraser with pressure put on it—manipulated." After doing these exercises, some children were more appreciative of their life, breath, and feelings and were happy that they were not inanimate objects. Other children responded that the exercises helped them be more adaptable and able to see something from another point of view: "I can see what I need to do when I need to speed up—become a ball." We gain interesting insights when we compare their responses to being a triangle with those being a ball or a cube. Some students saw a triangle as being levelheaded and strong, with a sturdy foundation and a sense of seriousness, while they saw a ball as constantly in motion and full of fun. A cube, they felt, would always land on one of its flat sides when turned; it would not be in constant motion like the balloon or cylinder.

Conversely, the shapes children don't want to be may relate to not wanting to experience their shadow. When children allow themselves to experience being the other and are encouraged to articulate their feelings about it, they may discover some of their reasons for their dislikes.

As guides, we help them to embark on an adventure into self-exploration and self-discovery. The information that children discover about themselves can assist them in getting along better with other people. The exercises on shape that follow will help children see how they fit into certain situations, as well as gain more insight into different aspects of their personality.

Exercise 206

Choose a shape you like.

Imagine you are this shape.

Tell what it is like to be this shape.

How do you feel?

What can you do?

Exercise 207

Choose a shape you don't like.

Imagine you are this shape.

Tell what it feels like to be this shape.

What don't you like about being this shape?

Exercise 208

See yourself as a cube.

How does it feel to be a cube?

Do you like it?

What material and what color are you?

What can you do?

Exercise 209

See yourself being a cylinder.

How do you like being a cylinder?

Tell what you are made of .

Tell what color you are.

What can you do being a cylinder that you couldn't do otherwise?

Exercise 210

Be a ball.

What kind of ball are you?

Tell what you can do being a ball.

Do you like being a ball?

If so, tell for what reasons.

If you don't like being a ball, tell the reasons for that.

Exercise 211

See yourself as a seashell.

What sort of seashell are you?

Exercise 212

Imagine you find a seashell on the beach.

Put it to your ear.

Hear the sound.

What is it saying?

What is happening?

Exercise 213

Be a rainbow in all its beautiful colors.

What do you sense and feel when you are a rainbow?

Exercise 214

Choose three things you want to be.

Tell what they are and why you want to be them.

Tell how it feels to be each one.

Exercise 215

Be three things you don't want to be.

What are these three things?

How does it feel to be these things?

Why don't you want to be these things?

Hats

The following hat exercises are good because they unite both color and shape in the form of a hat. A child can learn about the different facets of himself by wearing different hats, which will enable him to acquire a sense of how to interact with peers and family members. It is not difficult for a child to see himself changing his behavior to correspond to the hat he wears. And children enjoy imagining different hats.

Parents and teachers can use these exercises as a game whenever they want a child to behave in a particular way. They can ask him to see himself wearing a particular hat. These exercises are a fun way to bring out the best in a child, and if used consistently, they can create good habits in children. A child can do a different exercise from the following series on each day of the week.

This hat is the kindest hat in the world. It helps people. When I wear it the...

Exercise 216

See yourself in front of a box containing lots of different hats.

You pick one that you like, and you see written on it the word
  CONFIDENT.

Wearing this hat, you act the part for the day.

What are you doing?

What is happening?

How do you feel?

Exercise 217

See yourself choosing the hat of WISDOM.

What form and color is it?

Of what material is it made?

You put it on and immediately you know you have picked the hat
  of wisdom,

Because you begin to act wisely and you feel wise.

Describe what is happening, what you are doing, and how it feels.

You wish to keep this hat on

But you have absorbed the ingredients of wisdom.

And, in any case, you can always return to put on this hat again.

So now you see yourself exchanging it

For yet another hat.

Exercise 218

This time, you have chosen the hat of COURAGE.

You know this because you begin to act courageously.

Tell some of the courageous things you are doing.

What form and what color does this hat have?

Exercise 219

You are at the zoo and the doors around the cage open.

Because you are curious, you enter.

All of the animals begin to roar,

Every very wild animal together.

But you are not frightened because you are wearing the hat of
  courage

And you return quietly to the fields.

Because you are quiet, the beasts return to being quiet.

Exercise 220

It is now time for you to wear a different hat.

And you know as soon as you put it on,

That you have chosen the hat of GENEROSITY

Because you find yourself acting generously to all the people
  around you,

And you hear them saying how kind you are.

See what is happening.

What are you doing?

Child's Response

If I had courage I will not be afraid of anything. I might be scared
of a dinosaur. But I will not be scared of no one but maybe if it was

my mother screaming at me I might be scared. That is how I will
be if I had courage.

—Cindy, age 8

Masks

Experimentation with masks can be a very fruitful learning
experience for children, as you will see from the exercises that
follow. Children enjoy wearing different masks because it appeals
to their sense of fun and enjoyment of drama. Masquerading as
someone else satisfies their love of imagination. When they put
on a particular mask, they can imagine themselves in a particular
manner contrary to how they might normally act. For example, if
they put on the mask of confidence, they get to act confidently and
to experience the good feelings that confident behavior embodies.
These good feelings, in turn, become strong motivators for acting
in a desired manner, where otherwise one might have felt unequal
to the task. Thus, selectively wearing different masks can be a
powerful tool to change self-image.

Exercise 221

See yourself sitting at your desk.

In front of you there is a box.

You open it and see it is full of masks.

You pick a mask and put it on.

You have chosen the mask of SELF-CONTROL.

You know this because, as you put it on,

Your behavior in class and at home immediately improves.

You want to throw your lunch in the garbage,

But you eat it instead.

You want to go out and play

Instead of doing your homework,

But you do your homework first,

And then go out to play.

Notice all the other things that you are doing

Or not doing

When you wear the self-control mask.

Do you think you can control yourself enough

To put on this mask

Whenever you need it?

Tell about the many ways that wearing this mask

Improves your life.

Exercise 222

You are sitting at your desk with your box full of masks.

See yourself putting on the mask of HAPPINESS.

Now that you are wearing this mask,

You begin to see pictures in your mind

Of all the things and all the people that make you happy.

Tell who and what you are seeing.

If there is anybody you have left out,

Add them to the movie of your mind.

Breathe out.

Whenever you want to feel happy

Put on this happy mask.

And if you want somebody else to be happy

See them wearing the happy mask.

Exercise 223

Sit at your desk with your box of masks.

You pick the mask of FRIENDLINESS.

See yourself going about your day being friendly to everyone.

Yes I mean everyone!

Notice how everybody is behaving to you too.

Tell or write about your friendly day.

Exercise 224

Sit at your desk with a box full of masks.

Imagine you put on the mask of LOVE.

When you wear this mask, you do not hate anybody,

Including yourself.

Who and what are you loving?

Tell about some of the loving things you are doing.

Sense how good this makes you feel.

See, sense and know how good your love makes others feel.

And know that even a little love can go a long way.

Characters

It is good for children to experience characters outside their
everyday realm of being. Through exploring other characters,

particularly fairytale characters, children can get in touch with different aspects of their own personality: the courage and assertiveness they may be afraid to show; the sensitivity and caring they might push aside because it isn't "cool"; or the impishness and fun they can't let out because they must be too responsible for themselves or others. The following exercises will help children get in touch with the latent aspects inside of themselves.

Exercise 225

Imagine putting on the costume of Cinderella.

Go through your day being Cinderella.

What do you do?

How do you feel?

What is happening?

Exercise 226

Put on the costume of Peter Pan.

Spend your day being Peter Pan.

Tell what is happening and what it feels like.

Exercise 227

Put on the costume of Pinocchio.

Go about your day being Pinocchio.

What do you like about being Pinocchio?

What don't you like?

Describe your feelings and what is happening.

Exercise 228

This time put on the costume of Jack and the Beanstalk.

How does your day go being Jack and the Beanstalk.

What do you do?

Do you talk to anyone — if so, who?

Tell how you feel and what is happening.

Exercise 229

Put on the costume of the Tin Man in The Wizard of Oz.

Wear this costume and be this person all day long.

Tell what is happening and how you feel.

During the day you do something to get a heart.

Tell what you are doing.

Exercise 230

Put on the costume of the Wizard from The Wizard of Oz.

See and sense how it feels to be wearing this costume for one day.

Tell what is happening and how you like it.

Exercise 231

Put on the costume of the Cowardly Lion from The Wizard of Oz.

Imagine being a lion without courage.

What act of courage do you do

To become a lion with courage?

Exercise 232

What character in what book would you most like to be?

Tell why you would like to be this character.

What do you do and how do you feel as this character?

Emily
Age – 9
June 11, 2004

Dorothy –

I Like being dorothy
because I have nice
Friends. And I have a
Special dog. and I
have bueatiFul Shoes.
but the only thing I
hate is the bad
witch and her ugly birds.
and I Feel scared next
to the wicth.

Exercise 233

What character from a book or movie would you least like to be?

Give your reasons for choosing this character.

Describe your feelings and the feelings of the people around you.

Exercise 234

Be a good fairy.

What do you look like?

Describe it in detail.

What are you doing?

Breathe out.

Now be a bad fairy.

Describe in detail what you look like.

What are you doing?

Which do you prefer?

Being the good or the bad fairy?

Give the reasons for your answer.

Exercise 235

Have the bad fairy say something to the good fairy.

Now, have the good fairy say something to the bad fairy.

Hear clearly and tell what each is saying.

Exercise 236

Be an explorer excavating the ruins of an old castle.

What does it look like?

What do you feel?

What do you find?

Are you alone, or are you with someone?

Exercise 237

Be a sailor sailing from one port to another.

Which are the ports you are sailing to?

What do you see?

Where do you go?

What is happening that is interesting you?

Up and Down

Life is full of ups and downs, and it is important for children to learn how to balance their lives. The exercises in this section relate to internal mood changes as well as to external situations to which children commonly react. These external situations may affect their moods to a greater or lesser extent, depending on how they choose to see them. Practicing these exercises may help children develop internal resilience, as they learn to differentiate between being acted upon or simply being. In the following exercises, becoming the seesaw or the swing can add a level of perception. When children imagine themselves being the swing, they become the source of the movement as opposed to being the recipient. This awareness will help them gain a deeper understanding of responsibility, because they see the difference between being and doing.

Exercise 238

See yourself in the playground.

Describe everything that is in this playground.

Who is there with you?

What are you doing?

What is happening?

What are you feeling?

Exercise 239

You are sitting or standing on the swing.

How does it feel?

Now imagine you are the swing.

How is it to be the swing?

Exercise 240

Imagine you are sitting on the seesaw.

Who is sitting at the other end?

How does it feel to go up?

How does it feel to go down?

Exercise 241

See and sense yourself becoming the seesaw.

How is it to be the seesaw?

Exercise 242

See yourself on the merry-go-round.

Who else is on it with you?

How does it feel to be spinning round and round?

Exercise 243

See and sense yourself becoming the merry-go-round.

How do you like being the merry-go-round?

Exercise 244

Imagine you are standing on the top of a cliff

Looking down at the seashore below.

What do you see?

Exercise 245

See yourself climbing up and down a ladder.

How big is your ladder?

Where does it lead you to?

Tell what you feel when you go up

And tell what you feel when you go down.

Which do you prefer, going up or going down?

Give your reasons why.

Exercise 246

Imagine you are walking forwards.

Now imagine you are walking backwards.

Describe the different sensations

Walking forward and walking backward.

Animals

Most children are naturally interested in the animal kingdom, and it is not difficult for them to imagine being one particular animal or another. For them it is a game which gives them a sense of freedom, because breaking out of one's boundaries, even if only for a moment, is liberating. After returning to themselves they see, sense, and know themselves better.

In addition to gaining a sense of freedom and awareness, children can incorporate animal characteristics into their personality when they pretend they are a particular animal. For example, a timid child, or one who is a target for the bully, can imagine himself being a lion, and see himself acting with boldness and courage as he drives away his fear. The following exercises can help transform a child's natural tendencies, and allow for the growth of inner security and strength.

Exercise 247
Imagine you are an ant
Working diligently.
How does it feel to be
The smallest of creatures?

Exercise 248
Be a monkey
Swinging by your tail from twig to twig.
Sense how jumping from one twig to another twig
Changes your center of gravity,
Which permits you to be agile.
How does this feel?

Exercise 249
See yourself as a porcupine
And know that nothing can hurt you.

Know also that you are making space around you,
And sense how you feel well because you have made space.

Exercise 250

Be a giraffe talking to an ant,
What are you saying and what is the ant responding?
Breathe out.
Now be the ant talking to the giraffe
What are you saying and what is the giraffe responding?

Exercise 251

Imagine you are a bear in the forest
Foraging for food
How are you protecting your young ones?

Exercise 252

Be a camel surviving in the desert.
Know that during a long time
You will not eat or drink.
How do you feel?

Exercise 253

Be a fish
Swimming at the bottom of the ocean.
Now be a fish swimming at the surface.
What is the difference?
Which do you like better and for what reason?

Exercise 254

Be a squirrel,

Agile and nimble,
Gathering acorns in the summer
So you may eat in the winter.

Exercise 255
Be a lion
And sense how it is
To be king of all the animals.

Exercise 256
Be a cat
Sitting curled up
In somebody's lap.
Imagine you are telling a friend how this feels.

Exercise 257
Be an owl talking to a donkey.
What do you say to the donkey?
Now be a donkey talking to an owl.
What do you tell the owl?

Exercise 258
Play at being a scavenger
Groveling in the dirt for food.
Breathe out.
Now be an animal of prey
Stalking and seizing.
Breathe out.
Now be an animal that feeds off the grass.
See and sense how the ways of surviving are different.

Exercise 259

Choose to be one of the animals in the Garden of Eden
Having a conversation.
Choose the other one with whom you want to have a conversation.
What are you talking about?

Exercise 260

See yourself being a bat
Flying in the dark.
You are not frightened even though you are blind
Because you see by sensing.
You sense the obstacles so you don't crash into them
And arrive safely wherever you want to go.
Do you like being the bat?
What have you learned by being it?

Children's Responses

As a giraffe I feel too tall and very awkward. Sometimes people
make fun of me because I am very tall. On the other hand I
sometimes feel happy as a clown, because I am tall, and I can get a
lot of sunlight. When the rain falls I get the first drop. I also like to
bend over for people to pet me.

As an ant I feel sly as a fox sometimes because I can move fast and
get away with food particles, and I can also get away by running
into little cracks into the wall.

—Maryanne, age 12

I like to be a bear because it have fur so I don't have to be cold, and
I could sleep in a cave, and I could eat fish all the time, and when I
want I could go out and meet bears. I would feel so, so strong.

I hate to be a ant because I am small and people could step on me.

—Frantz, age 8

It feels bad to be a donkey because everyone hits you and think your stupid. And they say bad things about you. They make you pull heavy stuff because they're too lazy to pull it themselves.

—Harriet, age 10

I wish I was a bird because I could fly in the sky and it would feel like I am an airplane so I can go to any country I want to go, and I wouldn't have to pay. I will feel happy that I can visit my family. I don't like to be a lion because everybody will be afraid of me and I will be sad. And I don't like to be a lion. But a lion eats squirrels and other types of animals. I feel sick at the thought.

—Sherry, age 8

I dont want to be a skunk because I would stink and I wont have any friends.

Jean

age 9½

If the world was a world of animals I would be a ninja /cat because I can be a high jumper and I can enter the Animal Olympics. and I can protect people

P.S. See I won a silver cup

Ernest
10 years

I want to be a Dolphin Because They are very smart. And are fun to be around.

6
Creating the World You Want

*"I feel so fabulous when I think about creative
pictures in my mind. I always don't just make
the picture still in my head. I make the picture
move in action."*

—Randy, age 8

Exploring All Sides of Power

As with all things, power can be used in a negative or positive
manner. The right balance has to be found. Children who abnegate
their power will feel victimized. This may adversely affect their
ability to make choices. Should they make a choice, it may well
end up being damaging to themselves or others. Conversely,
children who have an exaggerated sense of their own power may
end up with relationship problems, due to aggressiveness and
intolerance of peers whom they perceive as weaker. The exercises
which follow the induction will help to nurture a balanced sense of
power in children.

At the start of each exercise, begin with the following induction:

"Sit comfortably in a chair with your legs uncrossed. Your hands
should be resting on your knees, palms up. Close your eyes and
keep them closed until I tell you to open them. This helps us see
things that we can't see with our eyes open. We will keep our eyes
closed no more than two minutes. Now breathe out slowly through
your mouth three times. Let me hear the sound of your breath
coming out of your mouth as you slowly release the air."

Note to Guide: Pause a couple of seconds to let the child finish breathing out, then begin with the exercise that you want the child to do. At the end of the exercise, pause very briefly and then say: "Breathe out once and open your eyes."

Becoming the King or Queen of Oneself

Exercise 261

You are the king or queen of a country.

What rules are you making?

What is happening?

What are the consequences for those who disobey your orders?

And what are the rewards for those who accept the rules?

Exercise 262

Now you are the subject of a despotic ruler.

Tell how it is to be the subject of such a ruler.

What can you do?

What can't you do?

How do you feel?

Exercise 263

You are the subject of a benign and kind ruler.

Tell how it is to be the subject of a kind ruler.

Tell what you are doing and how you are feeling.

Exercise 264

See yourself being the captain of a ship.

There is a mutiny aboard.

How are you managing to squash it,

And what is happening?

I am The Captain of A SHip

" I feel Very STRong. I am The
Big Man, The LeadeR, The
CapTain I have To Take
Responsibility FoR My
WoRKing, TalKing nicely
And Feeling. STRong and BRave,
ARound a lot of SailoRs
and lots of ocean, and
Dolphin, ShaRKS and Fish.
I Have a Big BoaT like
The Love BoaT.

Exercise 265

Be the pilot of a plane.

What kind of plane is it?

Where are you going?

Who is on the plane with you?

Do you like being a pilot of a plane?

Give your reasons for liking or not liking to be the pilot.

Exercise 266

Imagine you have in your hand a piece of clay.

Mold it to resemble your life till now.

Describe your sculpture.

Breathe out.

Mold it to resemble the life of your choice.

Breathe out.

Now mold it to resemble

How you want your life to be from now on.

Describe what you have created

At each stage.

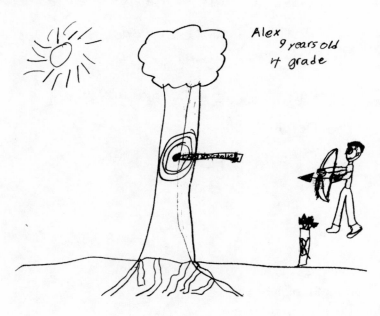

Alex
9 years old
4 grade

Exercise 267

You are in a large green meadow.

Choose a tree you like and walk over to it.

With a piece of white chalk in your hand,

Draw a circle on the trunk.

This is your target.

Now take five steps back.

Pick up your bow and arrow

124

And see your target.

Engrave your goal alongside the arrow.

Pay attention that your arrow, your eye, and the target

Are in a straight line.

When you see the line becoming a point

Release the arrow.

Watch where it falls

And you reach your goal,

If your eye, the arrow, and the center of the target

Are in a straight line becoming a point.

Exercise 268

If you don't know what your goal is

You may find it.

Have a bow and three arrows.

Release the arrows one at a time.

Now go and see where each has fallen.

Tell what you find at each place.

How You Use Your Power and Autonomy

Power is both a desire and a temptation for children. Although they don't fully understand power, they sense the feelings that accompany it when they have it and when they do not. When they hold the power, they also run the risk of abusing and misusing it. These exercises will help children learn how to be responsible when using power.

Exercise 269

You are the storekeeper of a little store.

Tell what kind of store it is.

What goods do you have in it?

Who comes by?

How do you like being the owner of this little store?

Exercise 270

You are the owner of a large supermarket.

You have many people working under you.

Tell what is happening and how you like it.

Exercise 271

You are the teacher for a day.

Tell what kind of a class you have.

Who are the children in this class?

Are they rowdy or quiet?

How are you getting them to do what you want?

Do you like being the teacher or do you prefer being the student?

Tell the reason for your answer.

Exercise 272

You are the principal of the school.

What kind of principal are you?

You hold a meeting with the teachers.

About what do you talk?

How is it different being a principal, a teacher, or a student?

Which do you prefer and why?

Exercise 273

Imagine yourself as the master of servants.

You assign jobs and tasks to each one.

Tell what is happening and how you are managing things.

What do you feel being the master?

Exercise 274

You are the traffic controller

Directing the traffic in a busy intersection

At a busy time of the day.

Tell what you are doing,

What is happening,

And how you like it.

An additional feature of power is that it is also concerned with mastery over oneself, be it through self-knowledge or self-control. For children, self-control runs counter to their natural way of being led by their instincts. These exercises are designed to help them become masters of themselves by using self-control.

Exercise 275

See your favorite meal in front of you.

Eat it fast.

Tell how it feels to eat your favorite meal fast.

Breathe out.

Now see yourself eating your favorite meal slowly.

How does it feel to eat it slowly?

Which do you prefer, eating it slowly or eating it fast?

Give your reasons in each case.

Exercise 276

See a meal you dislike in front of you.

But you are told you have to eat it.

How do you eat it?

How do you feel?

Exercise 277

See yourself being punished by your parent or a teacher.

You think it is unfair.

Tell what is happening

And how you are feeling.

What do you do?

Exercise 278

Imagine you are your teacher's favorite for one day.

Tell what is happening.

Do you like it?

Do the other children in the class like it?

Tell why or why not.

Exercise 279

Imagine you are your mother's or father's favorite for one day.

Tell what is happening.

Do you like it?

How do your brothers and sisters like it?

Tell what they are saying.

Taking Charge

Often, in order for children to change their reality about the world, they need to change their attitude or perception of the people and events around them. This will help children become more objective, and see other points of view. These exercises will help them do so.

Exercise 280

See yourself in a room

Full of masks and costumes.

You try on different masks and different costumes

Until you find one that fits you the best.

Describe what you are wearing.

How do you feel being this new person?

What can you do wearing this costume?

Exercise 281

Invite some members of your family into a room.

Help them choose costumes fitting for them.

Whom do you invite?

What costumes are they wearing?

If anything needs to be changed, change it now.

Exercise 282

Have all these characters interact with one another.

What is happening?

How do you feel?

Self-Confidence

If we were to isolate the one ingredient that deters us from being fully who we are, it would most likely be lack of self-confidence. That which distinguishes successful people from unsuccessful ones, amongst those of equal talent, is belief in oneself and in one's ability to achieve. Often we find less intelligent children more successful than more talented ones. When we observe why this is so, we see the answer lies in self-confidence. But this should not be cause for despair. Self-confidence is not dependent upon a gene:

it is something a child can acquire or destroy. The most common way a child can destroy self-confidence is by breaking agreements with himself. Being aware of this potential characteristic provides the key to building self-confidence. If a child wants to have self-confidence, he must keep the agreements he makes with himself. Should he need to, he can always readjust or redefine the those agreements.

The following exercises help the child identify the positive aspects of himself, which in turn build self-confidence.

Exercise 283

See and hear yourself describing yourself
To someone who doesn't know you.
What are you telling about yourself?

Exercise 284

See and hear yourself describing some of your characteristics
To an acquaintance.
What do you hear yourself telling?

Exercise 285

See and hear yourself telling someone you know well
At least three things that are special about you
And what is special about them.
Breathe out.
See yourself telling this person three things
You would like to change about yourself.
See yourself beginning to change one of them now.

Exercise 286

See yourself in the company of a friend who looks distinguished.
What is there about this person that makes them so distinguished?
Recognize and identify the essential features of this specialness.

Exercise 287

Make a list of all the things you couldn't do
A year ago,
Two years ago,
Three years ago.
Are there any of those things you can do now?
What happened to change it?

Exercise 288

What are some things you can't do now?
Are some of these things you would like to do?
Choose one and see and feel
What you are doing to make this happen.

Exercise 289

See yourself doing something easy.
What are you doing?
How do you feel?

Exercise 290

See yourself doing something difficult.
What are you doing?
How do you do it?
Do you ask somebody to help you?
How do you feel?

Exercise 291

See yourself wanting to succeed very badly at something specific.

It may be passing a test,

Making a friend,

Becoming a good basketball player,

Or anything else.

You set the time by when you achieve success,

And remember that the result has to happen in such a time.

Now see all the steps that you are taking to succeed.

The Opening Bud Series

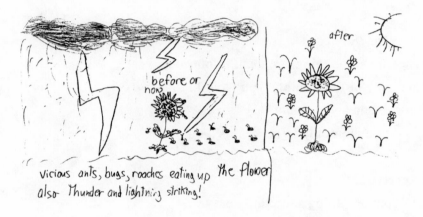

Vicious ants, bugs, roaches eating up the flower also Thunder and lightning striking!

Exercise 292

Imagine yourself as a bud that is very tightly closed.

Your petals are locked together and cannot open.

What is keeping the bud from blossoming?

How do you feel being this bud?

What are you saying?

What are the other flowers saying to you?

How do you look?

What shape and color are you?

Breathe out slowly three times.

See what is happening to make the bud open.

How do you feel as this opening flower?

What shape and color are you now?

Do you like being the opening flower?

Exercise 293

Be the most beautiful flower in a garden of beautiful flowers.

Tell what the garden looks like, what color the flowers are,

And what kind of flowers there are in this garden.

Tell what you look like: what shape, what size, what color, and
  what scent you have.

Exercise 294

Imagine you are a flower in a garden.

What do you say to the other flowers?

What do they say to you?

Hear the conversation clearly.

How do you feel being a flower in this garden?

Exercise 295

Be a flower turning into a fruit.

See and sense how the fruit is getting bigger and riper and sweeter.

What fruit are you?

Do you like it?

Give the reasons why.

Creating the World You Want

Now that children have experimented with power, it is time
for them to use it to create purely from their imagination. The
following exercises focus on letting children use the full reign of
their imagination in order to create the world they want.

Exercise 296

Close your eyes and breathe out slowly three times.

Paint a picture of things you want.

Make sure to put the main things you want in it.

Make sure you put yourself in it.

Tell what you are putting in your picture.

What colors are you using?

Breathe out slowly.

Open your eyes.

Now take crayon or pencil in hand, and actually draw your picture.

Exercise 297

Find something you wish would be different in your life now.

See yourself changing it.

What are you doing to change it?

Exercise 298

Make believe you are the most popular kid in the class.

Tell what is making you so popular.

Breathe out.

Make believe you are unpopular.

Tell what is making you unpopular.

Exercise 299

You are the scriptwriter and producer of a play.

You and your characters are about to perform.

See clearly each person's role.

Tell what your play is about.

What role do you choose for yourself?

Breathe out.

Do you like the way your play is unfolding?

Is there anything you wish to add, drop, or change?

If so, do it now.

Breathe out.

See also if you like the beginning and the ending.

Know that you can change any part you wish.

It is your play.

You are its creator.

Exercise 300

Go back into time

And live the period you would like to have lived in.

Who are you?

What century are you in?

What is happening?

Exercise 301

Go into the future.

What century have you chosen to live in this time?

Describe your world in detail.

Where and who are you in this world?

Exercise 302

Imagine you are looking at the angels.

See when you think a good thought

Or do a good deed,

They smile at one another.

What are you thinking or doing to make them smile at one
   another?

Breathe out slowly.

See how when you do something not worthy of you,

The angels look sad at each other.

Tell what is happening.

How do you feel?

Exercise 303

You are constructing a ladder

That takes you to a beautiful place

Where you want to be.

Describe this beautiful place.

Breathe out slowly.

See each time you do something of value

A rung is added to your ladder

That permits you to reach more easily the beautiful place.

Each time you do something unworthy

A rung gets loose or is broken.

Know there is always the possibility to repair.

Describe what is happening.

Exercise 304

Have a conversation with your pet.

You tell him how you feel.

What your hopes and secrets are.

What happened to you at school today.

Or anything else.

Hear what he is telling you in return,

And know why he is telling you these things.

Exercise 305

Be your pet.

How does it feel to be your pet?

Do you like it?

If so, tell the reasons why.

Exercise 306

Play a game where you are your pet

And yourself at the same time.

Do you like it?

What is happening?

Exercise 307

See yourself growing up to the first cloud in the sky.

You are now standing on top of the world.

Put your feet in the country where you

Think you will have the most fun.

Describe the fun you are having.

Now come down with the cloud.

See yourself traveling down some fast flowing waters.

You arrive at an encampment of Indians.

Tell how you are enjoying yourself

With the little Indian children.

Exercise 308

See yourself with a palette of paints in front of you.

See every conceivable color you want

And as much paper as you like.

With the colors that you like the best, draw your name.

Sound out the sound of your name as you are drawing.

Notice how it sounds.

Notice the colors you've used.

Notice the type of handwriting you've written.

See how you feel about your name.

Exercise 309

See yourself with a large canvas in front of you.

Draw the world as you see it in your present life.

Breathe out.

Notice what you've drawn and the colors you've used.

How do you feel about this painting?

Now open your eyes and concretely draw the picture.

Exercise 310

You have a piece of Play-Doh.

Create a model of a world you would like to see.

Describe your world and tell what you like about it.

At the Sea Series

The purpose of the "At the Sea Series" is to encourage children to explore the world around them, to expand their horizons, and to discover treasures wherever they find themselves.

I must go down to the seas again, to the lonely sea and the sky,

And all I ask is a tall ship and a star to steer her by,
And the wheel's kick and the wind's song and the white sail's
  shaking,
And a grey mist on the sea's face and a grey dawn breaking.

I must go down to the seas again, for the call of the running tide
Is a wild call and a clear call that may not be denied;
And all I ask is a windy day with the white clouds flying,
And the flung spray and the blown spume, and the sea-gulls crying.

—John Masefield

Exercise 311

Imagine you are at the seashore.
The sky is blue, not a cloud in view.
You are walking on the warm white sand
And feel your feet sinking.
At the edge of the water you sit down,
Dipping your feet in the blue, clear, cold water.
What is the sensation?

Exercise 312

You are sitting at the seashore collecting shells.
They are the kind that you put to your ear and listen to.
Take three of them.
Put them one at a time to your ear and listen.
Tell what each one says to you.

Exercise 313

See the horizon where the sky and the water seem to meet,
And know that this is land's end.

139

What do you see and what do you feel?

Breathe out.

You plunge into the water

And swim to a raft.

You climb onto the raft and float.

Tell what is happening and how you feel.

Exercise 314

A raft takes you to an undiscovered island.

You get out and begin to explore it.

Tell what it looks like, what you feel, and what you find.

Do you like this island?

Do you want to stay, or do you want to find your way back?

Exercise 315

You are on an island.

This island has a lot of treasures.

They are all for you but they are hidden.

Tell where you find them and what they are.

For what reason do you need these things now?

Exercise 316

In addition to treasure, this island is a land of Secrets and Mystery.

Tell the secrets and mysteries you have learned.

What will you do with this knowledge?

Exercise 317

You are on an island for a year and a day

Before deciding to leave.

Tell how you spend your time.

How do you leave and where do you leave for?

How does it feel to say goodbye to this place?

What have you learned from being on this island?

How are you different from when you came?

Children's Responses

I imagined that I was at the sea shore and I pick up a shell and put it by my ears. I heard I should learn better. The second shell said my mother is making chicken soup. The third shell said I am a big girl. I felt very happy about it. I learned I shouldn't keep secrets no more or hide them. Sometimes I hide secrets from my mother because I'm afraid. She might do something to my things. She might throw them away.

—Nana, age 10

I'm sitting at the seashore when I see three seashells. I put one to my ear and it says, "David, you need to be more serious." Says the first one. And the other one says, "We are the shells of virtues. You mustn't be a liar," says the second one. And then the third one says, "You must not be a violent person," says the shell. They disappear. Waiting for the next child to teach it its virtues.

—David, age 12

First shell says, "You have the ability to do what you want. You must not be lazy." Second shell says, "Life is a field of dreams. Dreams eventually come true. And when you set your mind to it, you can make your life a dream come true. Life is a dream succeeded." Third shells says, "Listen to the two other shells."

—Wendy, age 13

My world is round with lots of colors, like a ball of beautiful colors. My people are gentle, loving, understanding, and always caring. Flowers bloom in the month of June, and my bushes are covered with chocolate. There is always peace in my world, no guns, bandits, or drug dealers. Just the people of God. I feel peaceful, calm, and tranquil. Always there is the love of Nature in my world.

—Antoinette, age 13

Epilogue

Clarisse—A Success Story

As you can tell from many of the children's responses throughout the book, guided imagery has impacted children in powerful and positive ways. Perhaps one of the most striking examples of the positive effects of guided imagery, however, is found through the experience of a young girl named Clarisse.

Nine-year-old Clarisse was very much an outcast. She had no idea of personal hygiene and would come to school reeking of urine, unkempt, and in soiled clothes. Teachers refused to have her in their class for more than a week or two. Her peers constantly made nasty remarks about her. No one wanted to sit near her; no one wanted to play with her. She became extremely aggressive towards her teachers and classmates and was finally sent to me for counseling.

The first time I met her, I was shocked at the condition she was in. Indeed, in spite of opening the window wide in the bitter cold winter, her body smell was overpowering and gave me a throbbing headache. During the week after the session, I kept thinking about Clarisse. Should I buy her some nice perfumed soap and other toiletries, I wondered. Would she be pleased, or would she be offended if I did? Then I realized that those children who are hardest to love need loving the most.

The next week when I picked up Clarisse for her group session, I saw that nobody wanted to play with her and the name-calling was rampant. I decided to sit down beside her and played with her, interjecting words of praise as we played. It may have been the first time Clarisse received such treatment. Eventually I addressed the topic of personal hygiene with her, and each week afterwards, regardless of her appearance, I would find something about her to praise: she had pretty barrettes in her hair one week; the next, her dress was a lovely color. In addition, I engaged her in imagery exercises to improve her self-awareness and self-esteem. Within three to four weeks, Clarisse came in clean, well-kempt, and well-groomed. She so identified with me that when I guided her through the exercise of being a mountain, she drew two mountains side by side, actually touching each other, both red and both looking identical with their smiling faces. On one she wrote Miss Bezwiz—her form of Berkovits—and on the other she wrote Clarisse. She continued to practice personal hygiene, and her fighting and aggressive behavior decreased noticeably.

Clarisse was later heard to say about doing imagery exercises, "I like to dream—it's fun—instead of just thinking!" The "dreaming" she did in the imaging exercises changed her self-image and gave her self-respect.

Clarisse is living proof that when children are given the chance to explore themselves and their worlds through imagery, incredible transformations can take place!

Author's Note

I am very interested in hearing from my readers. Please forward your questions, reactions, and comments about what worked, what didn't work, and what you'd like to see in a forthcoming book to me, Sarah Berkovits, either via e-mail (ssb316@msn.com) or in hard copy by postal mail to myself in care of my publisher, Whole Person Associates, Inc. Kindly include a self-addressed, stamped envelope with your correspondence.

About the Author

Sarah Berkovits grew up in England, where she received her bachelor of education degree at the University of London, summa cum laude. After teaching for several years, she moved to New York and soon distinguished herself as an innovative and creative teacher at the prestigious Yeshiva of Flatbush. She taught there for five years before moving on to become assistant principal at The Shulamith School for Girls in Brooklyn. During this time, she earned her master's degree in education from Adelphi University. Subsequently, she became interested in the emotional development of the child and took up studies at the Postgraduate Center for Mental Health, one of the most acclaimed psychoanalytic institutes in New York City. Upon graduating, she proceeded to the doctoral program in counseling psychology at New York University.

Through her studies in imagery with Colette Aboulker-Muscat in the past twenty-three years, Ms. Berkovits saw the benefits of Madame Aboulker-Muscat's technique and adapted it for children. When the New York City Department of Education heard of her successes, they asked Ms. Berkovits to develop a curriculum in guided imagery and teach professionals in education. She is the person responsible for developing and bringing guided imagery into the classrooms of the five boroughs of New York City, as well as many schools in the tri-state area.

Ms. Berkovits currently conducts parent and teacher workshops in the United States, England, and Israel and is available for consultation to individuals and school systems. She also has a private psychotherapy practice and has published a number of short stories for children and adults.

Printed in the United States
70807LV00003B/226-324